FAMILY SCIENCE was made possible by **Chevron** a grant from the people of Chevron.

FAMILY SCIENCE

Editors
David Heil
Gayle Amorose
Anne Gurnee
Amy Harrison

Lead Developer
Peggy Noone

Other Contributors
Rhett Lewis
Tim Erickson
Ann Clark

Illustrator
Charlotte Lewis

For information about the FAMILY SCIENCE program or to order additional copies of this book, contact:

FAMILY SCIENCE
6420 SW Macadam Avenue, Suite 208
Portland, Oregon 97201
Tel: (503) 245-2102
Fax: (503) 245-2628

Credits:

Design: Economy Prepress, Portland, Oregon
Printer: Valley Printing, Portland, Oregon

These materials were prepared under a grant from Chevron to Portland State University. However, any opinions, findings, conclusions, or recommendations expressed herein are those of the authors and do not necessarily reflect the views of Chevron or Portland State University.

ISBN   0-87678-114-8

CONTENTS

Preface

When I first arrived at the Oregon Museum of Science & Industry (OMSI) in the early 1980's, the U.S. was just coming to grips with the country's shortcomings in science education. Too many children were turning away from science in school, and too many parents were feeling helpless to do anything about it. The numbers were especially sad for girls and minority youth who were often discouraged from studying science, under the misconception that there were no career options for them down the road. With science reform efforts now in motion to correct these shortcomings, the phrase "science for all" has been popularized as a slogan for the future and interest in science and technology careers is on the rise.

A decade before reform efforts were underway, the Lawrence Hall of Science, University of California, Berkeley created the EQUALS program to encourage young women and minority youth in science and mathematics. Prompted by the success of EQUALS in California, two Portland advocates for educational equity, Madeline Moore and Fred Rectanus, established a regional branch of EQUALS, called Northwest EQUALS, at OMSI in the mid-80's.

About this same time, a passionate and energetic early childhood specialist named Peggy Noone was hired to help guide OMSI's development of a new Discovery Space, a science learning environment for young children and their parents. Drawn together by their mutual interest in learning experiences for parents and children, Peggy and Madeline were soon collaborating on hands-on science workshops in community schools and church basements throughout Portland, and the seeds for FAMILY SCIENCE were sown.

The 80's were a time of extraordinary growth and creative program development at OMSI, and the Northwest EQUALS team contributed significantly to that excitement. The EQUALS organization took note of Madeline and Peggy's success in the science arena and encouraged them to take their family science outreach program nationwide. An alliance with the National Urban Coalition in Washington, DC was formed and Chevron agreed to fund development of the program along with compilation and printing of a book of activities. In 1988 Northwest EQUALS relocated to Portland State University and FAMILY SCIENCE was born!

In the years that followed, activities were developed, workshops were held across the country and the "family science" phrase started taking hold. Schools, churches, parent/teacher associations, and corporations began hosting family science events in their communities and the grassroots nature of the family science movement came into full bloom.

As more and more communities requested workshops and events, the service side of FAMILY SCIENCE was growing by leaps and bounds, yet progress on the FAMILY SCIENCE publication slowed. A few years into the project, Madeline Moore left PSU to explore new opportunities, and a series of personnel shifts and changes at Northwest EQUALS followed. Eventually, Peggy Noone also departed PSU, and FAMILY SCIENCE enthusiasts across the country were left to plan their workshops and classes with well-worn drafts of the early activities.

In 1998, my firm in Portland contacted PSU to request a copy of FAMILY SCIENCE for use in our educational work. After discussion with the University, we entered into a contract to complete the book and bring the initial development phase of the project to a close. With the family science movement in full swing, the need for a compilation of activities was greater than ever. On another level, completion of the publication became a personal priority. Having been party to the earliest discussions about the program and having worked closely with individuals from the original team, I viewed this FAMILY SCIENCE book as an important record of the creative energy and community spirit that initiated the family science movement in the first place, as well as a valuable resource for the future growth of that movement.

Research in recent years has pointed out clearly that children who do activities with their parents, build close relationships, and learn together will be happier, more self-confident in their own learning, and demonstrate a high level of emotional well-being. That alone might be reason enough to pick up FAMILY SCIENCE and begin exploring everyday science topics with children. Yet add to this the fact that FAMILY SCIENCE is full of inexpensive, hands-on activities that encourage cooperative problem-solving, highlight multicultural contributions and career opportunities for all learners, and help reinforce a child's school-based science experiences, and we quickly see why the family science movement has become so strong. Simply put, it works!

With the release of this book we celebrate the overall success of the FAMILY SCIENCE program. In addition, we proudly launch a new phase of this exciting parent/child learning movement because the book will undoubtedly stimulate even more workshops, community events and family science celebrations in the future. This is exactly what Madeline, Peggy, Chevron and all the people who worked on FAMILY SCIENCE envisioned when the project was initiated over a decade ago. So now, with this publication in hand, the real fun begins!

David Heil
June, 1999

Acknowledgements

Thousands of individuals and nearly a hundred organizations have contributed to the development of FAMILY SCIENCE. Over the years, the initial partners——Northwest EQUALS, National Urban Coalition, and Chevron—were joined by 74 community teams and thousands of educators and family members in 30 U.S. states and 3 additional countries. The support and guidance given to the project by so many is greatly appreciated.

Chevron's leadership and early support helped transform FAMILY SCIENCE from a great idea to an even greater national movement. Their initial grant funded the development, field testing and printing of this FAMILY SCIENCE publication. Special thanks to Tom Parkins at Chevron for his tireless advocacy for this project.

The National Urban Coalition of Washington DC blended equity, education, culture and community perspectives to help guide development of FAMILY SCIENCE. Many thanks to Rhett Lewis at the Coalition for his creative contributions to the activities and his commitment to the inclusive nature of FAMILY SCIENCE.

FAMILY SCIENCE is modeled after the popular FAMILY MATH series developed by the EQUALS program at the Lawrence Hall of Science, University of California, Berkeley. The early leadership that EQUALS provided in encouraging young women and minority youth in mathematics helped set the stage for a similar approach with science. Thanks to the entire EQUALS team for their generosity of ideas, contacts, lessons learned, and their ongoing promotion of FAMILY SCIENCE through their own network of educators and advocates.

FAMILY SCIENCE is truly the product of grassroots involvement by thousands of family members, educators and pilot site team leaders participating in FAMILY SCIENCE workshops and events across the country. While the FAMILY SCIENCE network will grow even more once this publication is released, the enthusiasm and commitment to family learning in science that was demonstrated by early participants in the movement is truly appreciated.

Thanks to the following friends and colleagues for their contributions and support:

Renee Anderson, Dean Azule, Scott Bowler, David Cox, Sherwin Davidson, Patty DeBerry, Virginia Dougherty, Jose Franco, Brenda Gomez, Margaret Greer, Anne Heimlich, Linda Hirschy, Bev Jacobs, Rosanna Mattingly, Joan Miller, Sandy Moffet, Robert Nicholas, Jackie Nissen, Cari Olmstead, Steve Plotnick, Fred Rectanus, John Rehm,

Jamie Reiser, Laurie Schmidt, Gwen Shusterman, Mike Stockstill, Tina Tau, Nga Tran, Joy Wallace, Brenetta Ward, Ron Ward, and Karen Yamamoto.

A special thanks to Madeline Moore, Deana Beane, Nancy Kreinberg, and Kim Lan Conradt for the beginning. And thanks to Bill Feyerherm of Portland State University for seeing the project through to completion.

FAMILY SCIENCE Pilot Sites

Families, educators and workshop leaders from 74 U.S. communities and 3 international sites field tested the activities and ideas in this book. We are grateful to the following sites and individuals for establishing pilot programs in their communities:

Organization/Location	Team Members
Sears Elem. School; Kenai, AK	Maggie Reidel, Yolanda Schrader
New Frontiers; Flagstaff, AZ	Carole Ferlazzo, Beverly Burns
New Frontiers; Tucson, AZ	Heather Alberts, Tim Wernette
Valle Del Sol, Inc.; Phoenix, AZ	Virginia Sterling, Al Moya
Thousand Oaks School; Berkeley, CA	Linda Leader-Picone, Joan Haefele
Markham School; Hayward, CA	Sherry Smith, Judy Opilowsky
Alameda Co., Office of Ed; Hayward, CA	Caroline Sly
Oakland Museum; Oakland, CA	Sandy Bredt, Molly Whiteley
Modesto Schools-Bilingual Dept.; Modesto, CA	Rafael Hurtado, Jane Manley
St. Paschal Baylon Elem. School; Oakland, CA	Roseann Colvig, Margaret Mahon
Glenview School; Oakland, CA	Carol Ross, Suzanne Kreidt
Girls Inc. of West Contra Costa; Richmond, CA	Audrey Goins, Isabel Emerson
Mira Vista School; Richmond, CA	Sue Ellen Raby, Stacia Cragholm
Washington Jr. H.S.; Salinas, CA	Margaret White, Lyn Rosen
Belle Air School; San Bruno, CA	Carolyn Gray, Linda Hilling, Holly Borchelt
Mission Reading Clinic; San Francisco, CA	Armida Contreras, Maritsa Espinoza
San Francisco Unified School Dist.; San Francisco, CA	Maria Santos, Bernard Farges
San Leandro Girls Inc.; San Leandro, CA	Carolyn Shanks, Joanne Lothrop
Stanford Mid-Peninsula Urban Coalition; Stanford, CA	Beverly Lawrence, Tracey Coan
Council Spanish Speaking; Stockton, CA	Dan Dunlap, Sylvia Casillas
Los Nogales Elem. School; Camarillo, CA	Bonnie Ng, Eileen Harrison
Delta Sigma Theta Alumnae Association; Long Beach, CA	Jacqueline Thompson, Erma Nichols
Martin Elem. School; Santa Ana, CA	Helen Matthews, Anita Ford
Lincoln School; Ventura, CA	Sharon Willebrand
Adams County School Dist. #12; Denver, CO	Steven Iona, Janet Iona
Weld County School Dist #6; Greeley, CO	Robert Stack, Becky Ramirez, Denise Hapeman
Science Museum of Connecticut; West Hardford, CT	Susan Johanson
Hartford Public Schools; Hartford, CT	Marcia Massey
West Extended Schools; Washington, DC	Henrietta Jones, Marilyn Morgan
Shiloh Baptist Church; Washington, DC	Constance Tate, Matilene Berryman
Operation Sisters United; Washington, DC	Eleanor Cox, Diane Ables
Girls Clubs of Delaware; Wilmington, DE	Dianne Vickery, Helen Henry
Space Coast Science Center; Melbourne, FL	Judith Law, Kathleen Menzies
Sister Clara Muhammad Elem.; Atlanta, GA	Fatimah K. Al-Amin, Folami Prescott
Mililani Waena Elem. School; Honolulu, HI	Joan Aluag, Gracie Aoki, Susan Yanagia
Plummer Elem. School; Worley, ID	Emogene J. Wienclaw
Dove, Inc.; Decatur, IL	Connie Requarth, Jan Pritts

Organization/Location	Team Members
Jefferson Parish P.S.S.; Harvey, LA	Marjorie King, Lynda Bonura
New Orleans Public Schools; New Orleans, LA	Levon LeBan, Nona Batiste
Springfield Public Schools; Springfield, MA	Heather Duncan, Vickie Walker
Lovely Lexington Terrace Elem.; Baltimore, MD	Vernita Smith, Joann Snead
Eastern Intermediate School; Silver Spring, MD	Sandra Walker, Pamela Prue
Programs for Educ. Opportunity, Univ. of Michigan; Ann Arbor, MI	Eleanor Linn, Martha Adler
Fellowship Chapel-STEP; Detroit, MI	Dolores Smith, Ronald Massey
Math Science Tech Ctr-Willard; Minneapolis, MN	Shirley King, Janice Wahl
Mississippi Creative Arts, Magnet Elem.; St. Paul, MN	Kathy Erno, Mary Knappmiller
Red School House; St. Paul, MN	Charles Batiste, Cherie Neima
Maxfield Science, Math & Tech. Magnet Sch.; St. Paul, MN	Celeste Carty, Judy Klatt
Hays/Lodgepole; Hays, MT	Minerva Allen, Camie Doney
Science Museums of Charlotte, Discovery Place; Charlotte, NC	Jim Henley, Susan Cline
Sharon Elem. School; Charlotte, NC	Kay Rogers, Annie Grier
Ranson Jr. H.S.; Charlotte, NC	Brenda Lanning, Brooksetta Davidson
N. Carolina Museum of Life And Science; Durham, NC	Carol Witherspoon, Annette Boykin
Webster Cooperative School; Englewood, NJ	Elisabeth Deyon, Stacie O'Keefe
Abyssinian Baptist Church; New York, NY	Kim Blackwell-Vinson, Delores Lipscomb
Delta Sigma Theta; Cleveland, OH	Arlene Prevost, Barbara Harris
Alsea School; Alsea, OR	Ann Clark, Linda Roland, Connie Ash
Dayton Grade School; Dayton, OR	Cori Chambers, Rebecca Knudeson
Confederated Tribes of Grand Ronde; Grand Ronde, OR	Dean Azule, Camille Van Vleet
Woodlawn School; Portland, OR	Jerry Jeli, Terry McKelvey
Black Educational Center; Portland, OR	Sharon Mitchell, Joyce Harris
Harriet Tubman Middle School; Portland, OR	Melanie Ramsey, Ken Krause
Hawthorn Elem. School; Sweet Home, OR	Shari Furtwangler, Nina Ingram
Tygh Valley Elem. School; Tygh Valley, OR	Charlie Little
Nellie Muir School; Woodburn, OR	Diana Allowitz, Marta Vasquez
John Moffet Elem. School; Philadelphia, PA	Carol Smythe
Unicoi Co. Board of Education; Erwin, TN	Brenda Hensley, June Manuel
Knox County Teacher Center; Knoxville, TN	Marti Richardson, Monty Howell
Organization of Christians Assisting People; Pt. Arthur, TX	Chester Levy, Jr., Marsha Thigpen
Education Service Dist., Region 20; San Antonio, TX	Linda Mason, Ben Freeman
Ridgefield School District; Ridgefield, WA	Ronald Ward, Sarah Riley
Central Area Girls Inc.; Seattle, WA	Brenetta Ward, Ann Ball Tarpchinoff
Robert M. LaFollette School; Milwaukee, WI	Christina Sylvester, Ella Hayes
Centro de la Communidad Unida; Milwaukee, WI	Oscar Mireles, Walter Sava
Wyoming Indian Elementary; Ethete, WY	John Laird, Richard Heryford
FAMILY SCIENCE-Australia; Melbourne, Australia	Susan Cumming
Fundacion Centro De La Ciencia y La Technologia; San Jose, Costa Rica	Alejandra Leon Castella
Teknikeus Hus; Lulea, Sweden	Ann-Gerd Erickson

What Is Family Science?

FAMILY SCIENCE is an informal science education program that gives parents and children an opportunity to work and learn together. Hands-on activities that use easy-to-find, inexpensive materials let families explore the ways in which science plays a role in daily life.

Parental involvement in FAMILY SCIENCE is key to the program's success. By showing an interest in science and making time to explore ideas and conduct simple investigations, parents can have a positive influence on children who may otherwise decide that science is too hard, too abstract, or boring. An added benefit of FAMILY SCIENCE activities is that they provide parents with a link to school science curriculum. Doing science at home opens the door to talk with kids about what they're learning in school and can help reinforce the idea that anyone can be a scientist.

Teachers, parents and others interested in promoting FAMILY SCIENCE in their community may want to hold an event based on the concepts and activities presented in this book (see Chapter 8 for more information). The format, location and scheduling of an event should respond to the needs of local communities or neighborhoods. During FAMILY SCIENCE events, parents and children work cooperatively in pairs and small groups to solve problems and "talk science." The hands-on activities provide fun experiences for the entire family that build skills, confidence and excitement about science learning.

What are the specific goals of FAMILY SCIENCE?

To make science more accessible to families by offering:

- a non-threatening, hands-on approach to learning scientific processes, concepts and themes.

- cooperative learning activities which develop problem-solving, questioning and communication skills.

- strategies for encouraging all students to pursue scientific study.

- opportunities for families to participate in group science activities.

To demonstrate the relationship between science education and future career choices by providing:

- activities that highlight the relevancy of science to daily life.

- a forum for guest presenters to share information with families about various jobs and how they relate to science.

- a historical perspective on science discoveries that highlight various contributions of people from different cultures.

To get parents more involved in their children's science education by encouraging:

- participation in informal learning activities which supplement children's formal school science experiences.

- parental interest and involvement with school science curriculum.

- families to do science activities at home using inexpensive and readily available materials.

- adults and children to be partners in learning.

CHAPTER 1
AT HOME WITH SCIENCE

A Learning Environment for Science

Whether you do them at home or in a class, FAMILY SCIENCE activities are meant to be enjoyed. There is no need for immediate mastery of ideas. There are no tests at the end of the chapters. You and your children can take your time, continue an activity as long as you are interested, try lots of new things, or focus on learning just a few concepts. FAMILY SCIENCE provides a wonderful opportunity to create an environment at home or school that makes science approachable and fun. Here are some ideas to consider as you and your family explore science together.

Encourage questions.

Asking questions is the beginning of self-motivated learning. Questions originate with curiosity, and satisfying our curiosity motivates us. Teach your children how to find answers to their questions: consult library books, surf the Web, or ask teachers or other experts. If you don't know the answers, don't worry. You can look for them along with your children. Sharing in the joy of discovery is a wonderful model for future learning.

One way to encourage children to ask questions is to ask them yourself. Pose questions that are open-ended, not just those with one-word or yes or no answers. Here are some examples:

- *What happened?*
- *What is your prediction?*
- *What should we try next?*
- *What will happen if...?*
- *How is this the same as...or different from...?*

Make science a hands-on experience.

Most children love to do experiments. Handling physical objects, doing laboratory work, and exploring in the field is part of what makes science interesting and fun. Scientific explanations sometimes conflict with the way children suppose things happen or work. Conducting experiments gives them the chance to test and witness evidence that may change their minds. Hands-on experiments allow children to use scientific methods to distinguish facts from opinions and misconceptions.

Practice using inquiry skills everyday.

Observing, comparing, measuring, recording, experimenting, analyzing, communicating, reporting, and formulating questions are all important skills related to inquiry-based learning. You and your children can practice using these skills together. For instance, cooking requires measurement, shopping involves comparison, and sharing the day's events uses communication.

Teach problem-solving skills.

Solving problems is part of everyone's daily life. Teach your children about how you solve problems. Some strategies you might use include: drawing a picture or diagram; writing about the problem; talking it over with a friend; finding an expert to offer advice; breaking the problem down into smaller, more manageable chunks; or brainstorming lists of options. Children who learn to work through problems and explore different solutions become more capable and confident adults.

Enjoy the creative side of science.

Science is a creative endeavor, and creativity can be a motivator, a source of enjoyment and something to share with others. Visualizing, combining objects in new ways, producing new uses for objects, solving problems and puzzles, fantasizing, pretending, dreaming, designing, and producing unusual ideas are all a part of science.

Spend time talking and listening to your children.

Children learn to read, reason, and understand things better when adults read, talk and listen to them. Storytelling, playing games, and daily conversations provide opportunities for learning from and about each other. You can encourage children's language development as you plan science activities together. Using new vocabulary, writing, verbal sharing and drawing pictures will help children explain their thinking and express their feelings in constructive ways.

Support and encourage your children as science learners.

Parents are their children's first and most influential teachers. By showing an interest in science, you'll build a positive attitude about science learning in your children. Many of your children's life-long interests and attitudes emerge in elementary school. Encourage their innate curiosity by providing them with science-related books or magazines, making things together, and helping them demonstrate their own ideas through words, models, pictures, and stories. Encourage your children to participate in extra math, science and computer activities, such as school clubs, fairs, after-school groups, or museum classes.

Encourage good study habits.

Showing interest in your children's homework sends the message that learning is important and you care about their progress. Encourage good study habits by helping them establish a regular time and space for study, allowing time for them to talk about what is happening in school, and checking homework assignments.

Use mathematics.

Science depends on mathematics, and math involves more than just numbers. Math activities include looking at patterns, problem-solving, and knowing when to add, subtract, multiply, or divide. Show your child how you use math every day in practical and creative situations.

Demonstrate how science improves the way we live.

Think of examples around the house that show science and technology in action. Go on a science scavenger hunt at home. As you look at household items, can you identify ways that science, math or technology played a role in their development? From the kitchen refrigerator to the basement furnace to the medicine in your cabinet, help children see how scientific study has led to a world of improvements. Support your children's interest in science and let them know that with proper training they too can help improve the quality of life for all people.

Make connections between schooling and career choices.

Start by telling your children about your work. They will learn more about you and about the contributions you make to your community. Talk with other people about their jobs. Suggest to teachers that parents give school presentations about their occupations. Learn what makes scientists' work different from other jobs and what education they need to do their work. Help your children make informed career decisions by locating career information and sharing it with them.

Provide access to tools for learning.

Calculators, computers, and other tools are useful for organizing information and solving problems. Children who know how to use these tools will be more successful in science and math. If these tools aren't available at home, check with your local library, school or community college to see what's available.

Challenge stereotypes about who does science.

Reading about, meeting and talking with scientists who are women or role models from diverse backgrounds opens doors to new opportunities for many children. It also challenges assumptions children have about cultural and gender-based stereotypes and develops positive attitudes about their ability to be science learners. A positive attitude toward oneself—a "can do" attitude—builds interest and willingness to try new things and increases the persistence and confidence needed for rigorous studies ahead.

Safe Learning

FAMILY SCIENCE is full of fun and challenging activities the whole family can do together. But before you start anything, think about safety at home, school and work. Create a safe environment by requiring everyone in the family to practice safe habits and model safe habits yourself.

Before starting any activity:

- Check the comfort level of all group members about safety.
- Designate an uncluttered, well-lit work area.
- Consider the age and experience of the group members.
- Read package labels, even the small print.
- Place first aid resources in a clearly visible location.
- Know the exit route and procedures for your location.
- Learn the correct use of tools and equipment.
- Anticipate any problems that may be caused by the activity.
- Write and have everyone understand and sign a safety contract.
- No eating or drinking during activities.
- Never use an open flame without adult supervision.
- Use care in handling sharp equipment or glass.
- Wear eye protection when using projectiles or small moving objects or mixing or heating liquids.
- Review safety rules prior to and at appropriate times during an activity.

After finishing:

- Dispose of substances or materials properly.
- Clean up work area.
- Check that all tools and equipment are in safe, working order.
- Wash hands.

Before beginning a FAMILY SCIENCE activity, review safety issues with all participants. If you are leading a FAMILY SCIENCE event you may want to use the *Safety Contract* on pages 182-183. The activities in FAMILY SCIENCE are designed to be safe and fun for you and your family. Now it's up to you to make sure that each activity is done safely!

CHAPTER 2
OPENERS

Openers

The collection of science activities in this section are called "Openers." Openers are designed as beginning activities. Hands-on, cooperative and fun, they encourage family members to experiment, tinker, and solve problems. When used at the beginning of FAMILY SCIENCE events, they also help early arrivals to "get going."

Using Openers in FAMILY SCIENCE Events

In general, openers require workspace, a copy of the directions, and some household items. The supplies are listed at the beginning of each activity. Paragraphs bordered with an arrow mark indicate explanatory information about the activity that can be hidden under flaps on a poster. Participants can uncover and read them after they've completed the opener to learn about the science behind the activity.

Move It

Rim Roll

- Put a marble in a bowl.
- Without touching the marble or lifting the bowl, can you make the marble roll around the side of the bowl?

It takes some kind of force to start an object moving. Move the bowl in circles on the table until the marble is rolling around the side of the bowl. Objects at rest tend to stay at rest and objects in motion tend to stay in motion unless acted on by an outside force. This property is called inertia. The inertia of the moving marble keeps it on the side of the bowl. People in a moving car also have inertia. When the car stops suddenly, they will keep moving forward unless they are wearing seat belts. This is why seat belts are so important. Seat belts help stop the forward movement.

Making Change

- Draw a line 8 inches (20 centimeters) long.
- Place 8 nickels on the line touching each other.
- Staying on the line, slide the first nickel in the row away from the other nickels.
- The challenge is to make space between the last nickel and the rest of the line. However, you can only touch the first nickel and you must stay on the line.
- What would you do if you wanted to move the last 2 or 3 nickels?

In this activity, you provide the energy when you hit the first nickel against the others. The energy from the hit is transferred through each coin until it reaches the last nickel. Since there are no nickels next to the last nickel to transfer the energy to, the energy moves the last nickel away from the line of coins.

Supplies
- *marble*
- *large bowl*
- *paper*
- *pencil*
- *ruler*
- *8 nickels*
- *small, empty plastic soft drink bottle with cap*
- *water*
- *mug*
- *playing card*
- *safety glasses recommended*

Over the Edge

- Fill a plastic bottle with water. Replace the lid.
- Place a sheet of paper on the table with about half of it hanging over the edge.
- Put the bottle on the table on top of the paper.
- Talk with your partner about how to remove the paper without touching the bottle. Try out your ideas. How many ways can you devise?

One way to remove the paper without touching the bottle is to hold the overhanging paper and give it a quick pull. Objects at rest tend to stay at rest unless acted on by an outside force. This property is called inertia. Objects resist movement even when you apply a force. In this case, the force from the quick pull does not act long enough to overcome the bottle's inertia. The bottle remains on the table. Here's another alternative: slowly pull the overhanging paper while you hit the table. Each time you hit the table the bottle is bounced off the table. When the bottle is in the air, the paper is free to be pulled.

Clink

- Set a playing card on top of a mug.
- Place a coin on the card centered over the mug's opening.
- Without lifting the card, the coin or the mug, drop the coin into the mug.

A quick hit to the card will move it. The coin has inertia. It is at rest. The coin stays in the same place, but the card is not there to hold it. Gravity causes the coin to drop into the mug.

Simple Work

Age:
5-13
Participants:
Group, Family, Pair

Pulley Predictions

- Cut a 12 inch (30 centimeter) length of string and put one end through the hole in a spool. (If there is thread on the spool, cover the thread with a wide piece of tape.)
- One person holds the 2 loose ends of the string with the spool between their hands.
- Cut another piece of string about 2 yards (1.8 meters) in length.
- Tie the 2-yard string to the bucket handle. Set the bucket on the floor under the spool.
- Wrap the loose end of the 2-yard string around the spool once.
- What will happen to the bucket if you pull the loose end of the 2-yard string down until it touches the floor?
- Add weight to the bucket and try again.

Supplies
- *string*
- *ruler*
- *scissors*
- *spool of thread*
- *tape*
- *bucket with handle*
- *paper clips*

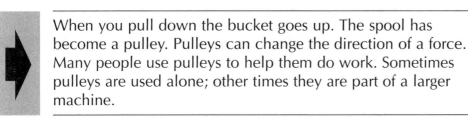

When you pull down the bucket goes up. The spool has become a pulley. Pulleys can change the direction of a force. Many people use pulleys to help them do work. Sometimes pulleys are used alone; other times they are part of a larger machine.

Paper Clip Work

- Open and straighten 3 paper clips.
- Bend the first paper clip so that it has a 3 inch (8 centimeter) jog in the center.
- Pinch one end between your fingers, while you turn the other end.
- Bend the second paper clip so that it has a 1/2 inch (1 centimeter) jog in the center.
- Hold one end, while you turn the other end.
- Leave the last paper clip straight.
- Pinch the end while turning the other end.
- Which is the hardest to turn? Which is the easiest?
- Describe to your partner what you notice about how each turns.

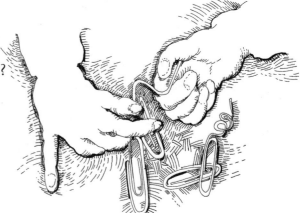

When turning or rotating something, there is always a trade-off between force and distance. In order to make work easier (exerting a smaller force), you'll have to push or pull further. When using the clip with the 3 inch jog, it took less force to rotate the wire, but you had to push or crank the wire further than with the other 2 clips.

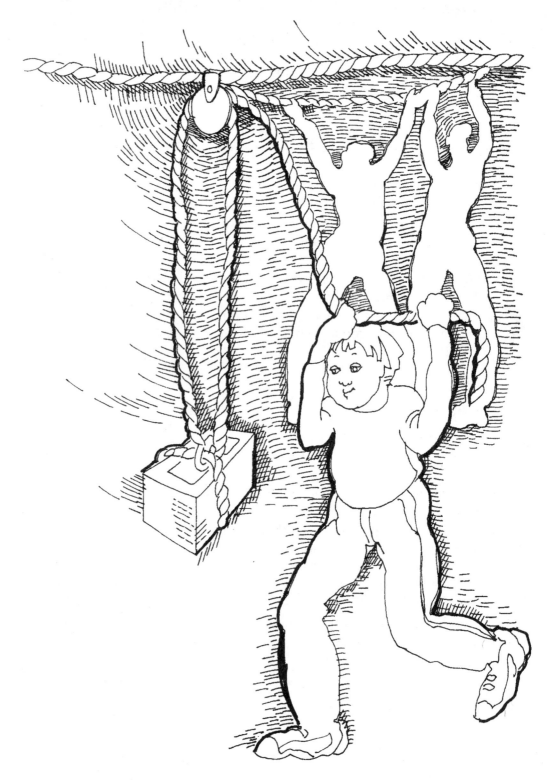

Attraction

Age:
5-13
Participants:
Group, Family, Pair

Find and Sort

- On a piece of paper, draw a chart with 2 columns. Label one side "attracted" and the other side "not attracted."
- Collect a group of small objects commonly found around your home.
- Find out whether the objects are attracted or not attracted to a magnet. Place the objects on the chart under the appropriate heading.

A magnet attracts objects that contain iron. Magnetism is a force that is used in telephones, radios, televisions, doorbells, electric motors, compasses, and numerous other inventions.

Along the Way

- Trace a paper clip on opposite sides of a paper plate.
- Draw a line that winds from one traced paper clip to the other.
- Put a paper clip on one of the drawings.
- Hold a magnet under the plate and paper clip.
- Use the magnet to move the paper clip along the line.
- Try other materials from your "attracted" and "not attracted" chart to take the place of the paper clip and paper plate.

The effect of a magnet can pass through non-magnetic materials.

Free to Move

- Find a few objects that are attracted to a magnet.
- Tape a ruler down on the table.
- Place one of the objects next to the end of the ruler. Place a magnet at the other end of the ruler.
- Slowly move the magnet closer until the object is pulled toward the magnet.
- Measure the distance between the magnet and object when the object began moving.
- Try again with a different object. After you have tested each item, compare the results.

Supplies

- *paper*
- *pen*
- *a collection of household objects (coins, paper clip, pen, staples, etc.)*
- *magnets, a variety of sizes*
- *pencil*
- *paper plate*
- *paper clip*
- *ruler*
- *tape*

- Try again holding the magnet above the object. Any difference in the measurement?

In this activity, you compare the force of the attraction between magnets and objects containing iron. The amount of iron in the object and the strength of the magnet affect the amount of the pull. The mass of the object also affects how easy it is to move.

Vibrations

Age:
5-13
Participants:
Group, Family, Pair

Sound Match

- One person fills 3 black film cans with a number of small objects so that each can makes a different sound when shaken.
- The other person tries to match the sounds by filling the other 3 film cans.

It Feels Right

- Rest your fingers gently on your throat.
- Say the word "vibration."
- Move your fingers along your throat until you find the spot where you feel the most vibration.
- Gently place your fingers on your partner's throat while he/she rests his/her fingers on yours. Talk about what you've discovered while you feel the vibrations on each other's throats.

A vibration is when something moves back and forth very fast. You will be able to feel the vibration and hear the sound at the same time. Different vibrating objects make different sounds. Can you feel the difference between the voice vibrations of an adult and a child?

Strumming

- Stretch a rubber band vertically around a mug, crossing the opening of the mug.
- Holding the bottom of the mug against your ear, pluck the rubber band.
- Add different sizes of rubber bands, and then pluck the rubber bands one at a time. Try strumming across all of the bands.
- Describe the sounds you hear to your partner.
- What would you do to the rubber bands if you wanted to change their sounds?

Sounds are produced when objects vibrate. You can produce different sounds by varying the tightness of the rubber bands. When stretched the same amount, a thin rubber band produces a higher pitch than a thick rubber band.

Supplies

- *6 film cans, black*
- *variety of objects to put in film cans (beans, popcorn, paper clips, confetti, etc.)*
- *rubber bands, variety of sizes*
- *small cup or mug*
- *tuning fork*
- *bowl*
- *water*

Quick Dip

(Note: Try borrowing a tuning fork from a local piano tuner, a music teacher, a choir director or a science teacher.)

- Hold the end of a tuning fork.
- Strike the tuning fork against the rubber sole of a shoe. Put it near your ear and listen.
- Strike it again, and then touch the tuning fork with your finger.
- Before you strike it again, predict what will happen if you put the vibrating tuning fork prongs in water. Talk about your ideas with someone else.
- Fill a bowl with water, and then try it.

The tuning fork starts vibrating when you strike it. Hold the tuning fork near your ear to listen and feel it moving. The size of the vibration changes according to how hard you strike the tuning fork. The pitch or frequency of a sound is measured by the number of vibrations that occur in one second. The more vibrations, the higher the pitch. The movement of the tuning fork is difficult to see until you put it in the water. The vibrating forks create waves and splashes in the water.

Going Down

Age:
5-13
Participants:
Group, Family, Pair

Playing Catch

- Cut out a newspaper rectangle.
- Hold it up in the air.
- Using only 2 fingers, have your partner try to catch the paper before it hits the ground. Let go when your partner is ready.
- What would you do to the paper if you wanted to catch it every time?

It is difficult to predict the movement of the paper. Air resistance slows its fall. The larger the surface area the more resistance the air offers the paper. The shape and orientation of the paper in the air guides the movement.

Handmade Spinners

- Trace the outline of your hand—palm down, thumb and fingers together—on a sheet of paper.
- Cut it out. Fold it in half lengthwise.
- Starting at the fingers, cut halfway up the fold.
- Roll the palm up until it meets the cut. Hold it in place with a paper clip.
- Fold one finger section forward and the other section back.
- Hold it above your head and drop it.
- Adjust the finger or palm section until it spins when you drop it.
- Try to change the direction and the speed that the spinner spins. Can you predict where the spinner will land?

The paper clip acts as a ballast on your spinner. A ballast is weight added to increase stability. Your spinner may remind you of a propeller. A propeller is a mechanical device with 2 or more blades twisted to create a spiral path as it rotates. Propellers propel planes or boats by pushing air or water backwards, which causes the craft to move forward. Before the civil war Benjamin T. Montgomery, a slave, invented a propeller for ocean vessels. Unfortunately, he was unable to obtain a patent because of a national ban on slaves receiving patents.

Supplies

- *scissors*
- *newspaper*
- *pencil*
- *paper*
- *paper clips*
- *2 balloons, the same size*
- *2 small plastic containers with lids, the same size*
- *coins*
- *tape*

Balloon Race

- Inflate a balloon to its largest size and tie the end.
- Inflate another balloon to half the size of the first. Tie the end.
- Stretch out your arms with a balloon in each hand.
- Before you let go, talk with your partner and predict which balloon will touch the floor first.
- Drop the balloons at the same time from the same height. Which one wins the race?

The air offers resistance to the balloons as they fall, slowing them down. The larger balloon has more resistance as it drops. Without air resistance all objects would fall at the same rate, no matter what their weight or size. Balloons used in astronomy are high altitude balloons that use telescopes to photograph the sun, planets, and other astronomical features. Broken balloon pieces can be harmful to living things—people, pets, birds and animals. Collect broken pieces and put them in the trash.

Heavy and Empty

- Start with 2 identical small plastic containers with lids.
- Fill one of the containers with coins, and then tape on the lid. Leave the second container empty and tape on its lid.
- Talk with your partner about what will happen when you drop both containers at the same time from the same height.
- Make a landing spot with a stack of newspaper.
- Before you drop the containers, predict which one will hit the ground first.
- One person drops the containers, while the other person stands back to watch which hits first.

An object's fall can be affected by air resistance. Without air resistance, all objects would fall at the same rate no matter what their weight or size. The two containers are the same size but different weights. Because the air resistance is the same on each, they hit the floor at the same time. Of course, you want to make sure that you are holding them at the same height and let go of them at the same time.

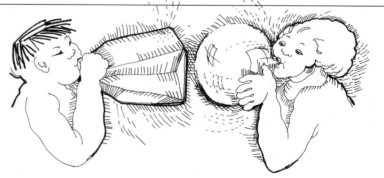

Air Lift

Age:
5-13
Participants:
Group, Family, Pair

Paper Wing

- Cut a strip of paper 1 inch by 6 inches (2.5 by 15 centimeters).
- Hold one end of the paper strip just below your bottom lip.
- Predict which direction the paper will move when you blow. Now give it a try.
- Change the size of the paper and the amount of air you blow.
- Compare what happens.

Blowing air over the paper decreases the air pressure on top. The air pressure under the paper doesn't change, so it pushes the paper up. This demonstrates what happens on an airplane wing. On an airplane, the curved surface of the wing causes the air to move faster over the top of the wing which lowers the air pressure. Because the air pressure is greater under the wings, the wings are pushed upward.

The Bridge

- Fold in the short sides of an index card 3/4 inch (2 centimeters).
- Set it down with the short sides touching the table so that it looks like a low bridge.
- What do you think will happen to the card when you blow under the bridge?
- Talk with your partner about your ideas, and then try it.

The card won't blow away. You have demonstrated what Daniel Bernoulli observed in the 18th century. The pressure is lowest where air is moving the fastest. The faster moving air below the card has lower pressure than the air above the card, so the card doesn't move. This is known as Bernoulli's principle. An airplane wing also demonstrates Bernoulli's principle. The airplane wing is shaped so that the air travels farther and faster across the top of the wing. The air moving across the top of the wing has lower pressure. The slower moving air below the wing has higher pressure and pushes the airplane wing up.

Supplies

- *paper*
- *scissors*
- *ruler*
- *index card*
- *pencil*
- *sheet of newspaper*
- *tape*
- *cotton ball*
- *2 balloons, the same size*
- *string, 1 yard or meter*

Cotton Cone

- Cut a square from a piece of newspaper that is at least 6 by 6 inches (15 by 15 centimeters).
- Roll the paper into a cone with a small opening on one end and a large opening on the other. Secure the cone with a piece of tape.
- Hold the cone with the large opening up. Drop in a cotton ball.
- Can you blow the cotton ball out of the paper cone through the small opening?
- Make a list of the ideas you and your partner have about how to do it, and then try it.
- Make a larger or smaller cone or ball, and then try it again.
- Compare what happens.

 To solve this problem, pinch closed the opening at the base of the funnel with your finger. Hold the funnel upright and blow into the wide opening. Now, by blowing into the funnel, you cause the pressure on the bottom of the cotton ball to be greater so that the cotton ball can be pushed out.

Swinging Balloons

- Inflate 2 balloons until they are the same size and tie them closed.
- Tie each end of a 1 yard (1 meter) string to each balloon.
- Hold the string so that the balloons hang about 8 inches (20 centimeters) apart.
- Predict what will happen when you blow between the balloons. Try it!

 Fast moving air has lower pressure than slow moving air. The balloons move closer together because the air pressure on the outer side of the balloons will be greater than the air pressure between the balloons.

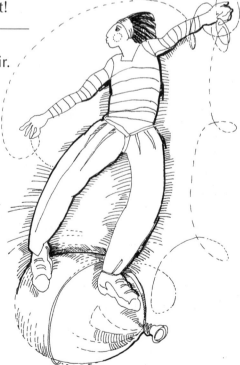

Time To Learn

Second Chance

- Copy and cut apart the 4, "L" pattern pieces (see page 37).
- Open the bottom and the side of a cereal box and flatten it.
- Trace the 4 pattern pieces onto the box, and cut them out.
- Record your time as you arrange the 4 triangles to form the letter L. The horizontal and vertical parts of the L will be the same widths but different lengths.
- Scramble the pattern pieces and repeat.
- Let your partner try it. Talk about the difference between your first and second tries.
- Estimate how long it would take you to do the puzzle a third time.

Human beings are very good at recognizing patterns. In fact, there has not been a computer invented to date that's as good at pattern recognition as the human brain. However, we do improve with practice. The more you practice a skill, the better or faster you become. Did your time for solving the "L" pattern puzzle decrease with practice?

Supplies

- *copy of the "L" Patterns*
- *empty cereal box*
- *pencil*
- *scissors*
- *clock with a second hand*
- *paper*
- *ruler*
- *string, at least 1 yard or meter*

Quick Copies

- Copy the paragraph below as fast as you can. Don't cross the t's or dot the i's. Have a partner time how long it takes you, and then switch.

  The Place of Stones, an astronomical observatory, was discovered in Kenya, Africa. At this prehistoric site, 19 stones were placed to match 7 constellations. Africans created accurate calendars by observing the location of the stars in the sky.

- Check your paragraph for crossed t's and dotted i's.
- Talk with your partner about what happened.

Crossing t's and dotting i's is a habit. We do it without thinking about it. It takes longer to not do it than it takes to do it. Good habits can improve our work at school, home, or on the job. What habits do you have that save time, energy or improve your work?

"L" Patterns

Cut apart on the lines to create
four triangles for each puzzle.

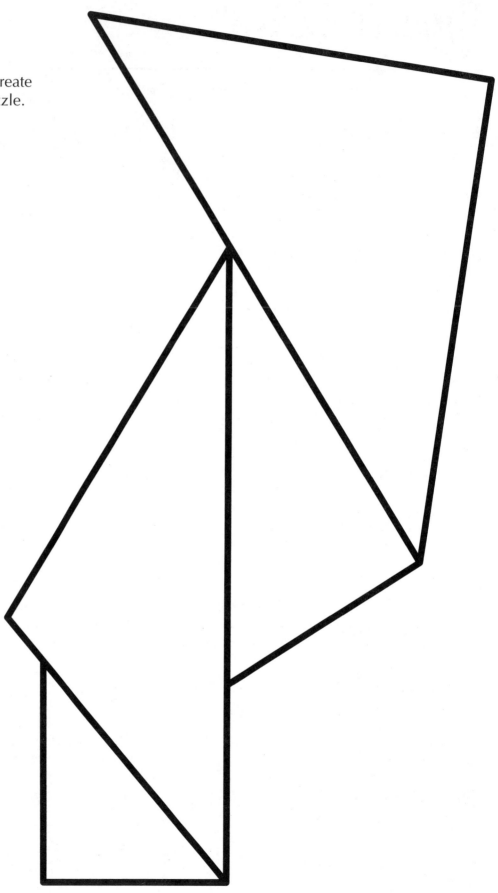

FAMILY SCIENCE

Balanced Bodies

Age:
5-13
Participants:
Group, Family, Pair

Forehead Rest

- Stand an arm's length away from a wall. Put your feet together.
- Using your arms for support, rest your forehead against the wall. Put your arms at your sides.
- Try to stand up right without bending your knees or hips, or moving your arms.

When you stand, your center of gravity is near the center of your torso, directly above your body's support, your feet. When you lean forward, your center of gravity changes position, moving to a spot under the upper part of your body. You can't stand up without bending your knees, hips, or moving your arms because you need to shift your center of gravity back over your feet to stay balanced.

Supplies

- *sheet of paper*

Shoulder Hold

- Hold a sheet of paper against the wall with one shoulder.
- Place your inside foot against the wall.
- Try to lift your outside foot without dropping the paper.

It is impossible to lift your foot because you have to move your body toward the wall to stay balanced. Have you ever lifted a heavy pail with one hand? You leaned away from the pail while you lifted. What would happen if you didn't lean?

Bender

- Stand against a wall with your heels touching it.
- Place a sheet of paper on the floor in front of you.
- Without moving your feet or bending your knees, try to pick up the paper.

Your feet are under your center of gravity when you stand. To bend forward, you have to move your hips backwards so that your center of gravity stays over your feet. Step away from the wall, bend over, and ask someone to describe the adjustments your body makes to stay balanced. What happens to your legs or hips? Step against the wall, and try again. What happens?

Moving Water

Supplies

- *permanent pen*
- *picnic plate, plastic or plastic coated*
- *water*
- *eye dropper*
- *paper towel*
- *plastic cups*
- *string*
- *ruler*

Water Drop Trails

- Draw 2 circles smaller than a dime on one side of a plastic plate.
- With a permanent pen, draw a straight, wavy, jagged, or curved line to connect the circles.
- Fill one circle with water from a dropper.
- By carefully tilting the plate, move the water drop along the line to the other circle.
- Dry off the plate with a paper towel, and then try again.
- Draw a new line or trade with a partner.

If you look at the water drop from the side, you'll see it has a dome-shaped top. When you start tipping the plate, the water drop stretches out as it moves, but it doesn't break apart. The phenomenon that holds the drop together is called surface tension.

Supply Line

- Fill a cup with water.
- Cut a length of string about 16 inches (40 centimeters) long.
- With a partner, devise a way to use the string to transfer the water from the full cup to an empty cup. Do not hold the full cup directly over the empty cup.

Usually when you pour from a container, gravity does the work for you, pulling the liquid straight down. You've been challenged to defy gravity. You can take advantage of the water's attraction to the string and it's tendency to stick to itself. Wet the string. Hold it against the lower edge of the cup. Pull the string as tight as you can, guiding the free end of the string over the empty cup. Now slowly begin to pour the water from one cup down the string to the other. The stream of water coming from the cup has a strong surface film around it. This film holds the water to the string. Because of water's strong surface tension, the string guides the path of the water into the cup, preventing it from dropping straight below. People who work in laboratories use this principle when they pour a solution from one container to another and must not spill a single drop. They will place a glass rod across the spout of their pouring container and let the solution run along the rod into the other container.

Wet and Dry

Age:
5-13
Participants:
Group, Family, Pair

Toothpick Star

- Bend 5 toothpicks in half without breaking them in two. Each will look like a "V."
- On a waterproof surface, arrange the 5 toothpicks with the points of the V's touching. It will look like a flower.
- Put the end of the straw in water.
- Place your finger over the end of the straw and lift it out of the water.
- What do you think will happen if you drop water in the center of the toothpick flower? Holding the straw over the center, lift your finger to drop water.

The wooden toothpicks absorb water through their broken ends. The wood fibers swell, forcing the toothpicks to straighten. The toothpick flower changes to a toothpick star.

Supplies

- *flat toothpicks*
- *plastic straw or eye dropper*
- *cup*
- *water*
- *ruler*
- *pencil*
- *paper*
- *scissors*

Folds Together

- Cut 2 paper strips about 1 inch by 2 inches (2.5 by 5 centimeters).
- Fold each strip in half lengthwise.
- Lay the strips on a waterproof surface with the folded edges touching.
- Discuss what will happen when you drop water where the folded edges touch.
- Try it.
- Compare what happens with different lengths and widths of paper.

When the paper absorbs the water, the paper fibers increase in size. This causes the paper to move. What is the largest size of paper that will move when water is added?

Wet Surfaces

Supplies

- *eye dropper*
- *water*
- *bottle cap*
- *small bowl*
- *roll of toilet paper*
- *paper clip*
- *toothpick*

Over the Top

- Fill the dropper with water.
- Hold the dropper over the bottle cap.
- Guess how many drops of water the bottle cap will hold.
- Count the drops as they fill the cap.

When the water reaches the rim of the cap, you may want to stop. However, you can add more water to the cap. As the water begins to go above the rim, look at the water from the side. The water surface is dome-shaped. Water's ability to hold together like this is due to its strong surface tension.

Paper Clip Raft

- Fill a bowl with water.
- Tear off one square of toilet paper.
- Float the paper clip in the bowl of water using only the square of toilet paper.

Place a paper clip on the toilet paper. Lift the paper and carefully lay it on the surface of the water. The toilet paper will sink and the paper clip will float. Look carefully at the water surface around the paper clip. What do you see? The surface tension of the water keeps the paper clip afloat.

Centering

- Fill a bowl with water.
- Drop in a toothpick.
- Can you make the toothpick float in the center of the bowl?

Water clings to the sides of containers. When you put the toothpick in the water, it floats along the side. The water level is highest there due to capillary action. Capillary action is the result of a liquid's attraction to the sides of a container and the liquid's surface tension. In this activity, you can change the highest point by adding water. When the water domes above the bowl's rim, the toothpick will float to the center.

Stoppers

Age:
5-13
Participants:
Group, Family, Pair

Spigot

- Using a nail, or the point of a pair of scissors, have an adult poke a small hole in the side of a plastic bottle near the bottom.
- Hold your finger over the hole while you fill the bottle with water.
- Screw on the cap. Remove your finger.
- Can you control when the water flows out of the hole?
- Talk with someone about how this would be useful.

You expect the water to leak out of the hole, but the cap keeps the outside air from pushing the water out of the bottle. When you remove the cap, air takes the place of the water as it flows out of the hole. Screwing on the lid again stops the flow of air into the bottle, and the water stops flowing out. As long as air can take the place of water, it will continue to flow.

Halfway

- Put a little water in a bottle.
- Place a cup upside-down on top of the open bottle. The top of the bottle should touch the bottom of the cup.
- Hold the cup against the bottle top, and then turn them both over.
- What would happen if you lifted the bottle half-way out of the cup?

Air enters the bottle when you lift it. The water flows out as the air moves in. When the water level in the cup reaches the opening of the bottle, it stops air from entering the bottle. When the air stops entering the bottle, the water stops flowing out.

Supplies

- *small nail or scissors*
- *2 clear plastic soft drink bottles with caps*
- *water*
- *wide mouth plastic cup*
- *heavy paper*
- *bucket*

Paper Lids

- Fill a cup with water.
- Cover the top of the cup with a sheet of heavy paper.
- Working over a bucket or sink, press your hand against the paper and turn the cup over.
- Carefully remove your hand from the paper.

Air pressure holds the paper in place. As you turn over the cup, a small amount of water will escape. Since just a little water escapes and no air (if you have made a good seal), the air pressure in the cup decreases. The higher air pressure outside the cup holds the paper against the rim.

Great Openings

Slots

- Collect at least 5 small household items.
- Choose 3 from your collection.
- What is the smallest opening you can cut in a piece of paper so that all 3 items will fit through it?
- Once you've cut your hole, return the 3 items to the collection.
- Give your partners the paper with the opening. Challenge them to find the 3 items you used.

35 Sense

- Trace a dime onto an index card. Cut out the circle.
- Without tearing the paper, put a quarter through the dime-size hole.

Although it doesn't seem possible, a quarter will fit through the dime-size hole. Hold the quarter perpendicular to the paper, and gently push the quarter through on edge while bending the card. Bending the card stretches the hole just enough to allow the quarter to pass through.

Hole In One

- Cut an opening in an index card large enough to fit your head through. It should have 2 closed ends.
- Can you cut an opening large enough to fit over a family member from head to toe?

There is more than one solution to this problem. Here's one way to solve it. Start by folding the index card in half. Next, cut very thin slits in the card as shown below (a), stopping approximately 1/4 inch from the edge. Be careful not to cut all the way through! Then cut open along the folded edge on all the slits (b) except the first and last. Carefully open up your paper "hole" and step through!

Supplies

- *a variety of small household items*
- *paper*
- *scissors*
- *dime and quarter*
- *index cards*
- *pencil*

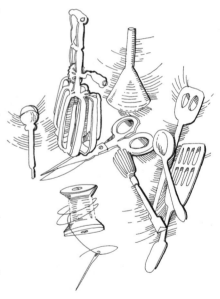

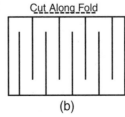

(a)   (b)

Challenging Structures

Supplies

- *3 empty cans, the same size*
- *2 sheets of paper, 81/2 x 11 inches*
- *3 pencils about the same size*
- *4 plastic cups, the same size*
- *handful of craft sticks*
- *empty cereal box*

Stack

- Set 2 cans on a flat surface. They must be far enough apart so that the third can't bridge between them.
- Use one sheet of paper to support the third can above the other 2.

Trivet

- Use 3 pencils to keep a can from touching the table.
- The pencil points can't touch the table or the can.

Platform

- Position 3 plastic cups to form a triangle. They must be far enough apart so that a craft stick will not bridge across any 2.
- Using 3 sticks, build a platform to hold the fourth cup above the first 3.

Breakfast Lift

- Using one sheet of paper, build a structure to raise an empty cereal box at least 4 inches (10 centimeters) off the table.
- The structure must support the box when you let go and move away from the table.

There is more than one solution to this problem. One solution is a tube. A tube is a strong, lightweight structure. It is a familiar form in both nature and technology. Plant stems, bamboo, pipes, columns and pillars are all types of tubes. What might be another solution?

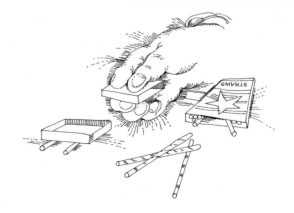

CHAPTER 3
SCIENCE AT WORK

Drawing From Experience

Supplies

- *pencil*
- *felt pens or crayons*
- *paper*

Why

To challenge our perceptions of scientists and their work.

What

A stereotype is an overly generalized concept or belief. Statements like "only women are nurses and only men are doctors" reinforce stereotypes. Children's future career choices expand when they're introduced to workers who challenge stereotypes. From astronaut to zoologist, girls and boys have an equal number of career choices. It is preparation and determination that build a career, not gender or race.

Support and encouragement from adults can make a difference as children prepare for the future. Also, providing examples of people and activities that challenge career stereotypes can make children more aware of their choices.

How

What image comes to mind when you think of a scientist?

- Each participant should draw a picture of a scientist.

- Everyone exchanges pictures and makes a list of everything they can tell about each scientist just by looking at the picture.

- When finished, participants share the items on their lists.

- Now have everyone look at their own picture. Pose the following questions:
  How did you decide what to draw?
  Would you like to meet the scientist in your picture?
  What area of science is your scientist interested in?
  How many years did he/she spend in school?
  Where does your scientist live? Does he/she have a family?
  Can you describe the place where your scientist works?

Next

- Collect current magazines and daily newspapers. Predict how long it will take for you to find information about a real scientist in the material you've collected. Divide into teams and race to find the first or the most information.

Did You Know...

Concern for the environment is not a new idea. Ellen Swallow Richards (1842-1911), a chemist, worked throughout her career to improve the quality of life at home and work. With a focus on ecology, she researched water purity, sanitation and pollutants in home products. In 1873, she was the first woman to graduate from Massachusetts Institute of Technology (M.I.T.).

Trios

Why

To appreciate the historical contributions of various individuals and cultures to science.

What

Through studying history, we can appreciate the diversity of people who have shared their ideas, solved problems and contributed to our understanding of the world. These historical perspectives can inspire us as we meet future scientific challenges.

How

In this activity, groups of 3 or more cooperatively tell historical science stories.

- Make copies of the *Science Story* cards (see pages 52-53), and then cut the cards apart. There are 6 cards in each set. Use one set for less than 6 people, or both sets for 6 to 12 people.

- Distribute the cards to the group. Each person needs at least one card. On each card there is one sentence from 3 different stories. The position of the sentence in a story is marked on the card.

- Decide who will read his/her first sentence. The person with the second sentence continues the story, and the third person finishes the story. Listen to the story being told to add your sentence at the correct time to the right story.

- Retell the story to check the order and accuracy of the sentences.

- Continue telling stories with each person having a turn to start by reading the first sentence on his/her card.

Next

- These science stories are just a beginning. If one story interests you, check the library or browse the Internet to find out more about the person or group in the story.

- After a trip to the library, have each family member write three sentences about another historic contribution to science. Separate your sentences to make a new set of *Science Story* cards.

••SCIENCE STORY••

First Sentence
Over 700 years ago, the Dogon people, who lived on the West Coast of Africa, had an enormous store of celestial knowledge.

Second Sentence
In September of 1980, he spent 7 days on the Salyut 6 Lab.

Third Sentence
She was the valedictorian of her graduating class at the New York Medical College for Women.

••SCIENCE STORY••

First Sentence
Earl Shaw was the son of sharecroppers.

Second Sentence
They studied the nature of creation from the stars to the formation of the planets.

Third Sentence
The horticultural practices of American Indians were more advanced than those of European farmers of the same period.

••SCIENCE STORY••

First Sentence
Arnaldo Tamayo Mendez, a Cuban cosmonaut, was the first person of color to go into space.

Second Sentence
His education began in a three-room school, but he went on to earn a Bachelor's degree, Master's degree, and a Ph.D. in physics.

Third Sentence
Modern astronomy has confirmed the findings of the Dogon people, including the spiral structure of the Milky Way, the moons around Jupiter, and the elliptical orbit of the Sirius system.

••SCIENCE STORY••

First Sentence
In North America, indigenous people used more than 2,000 species of plants for food.

Second Sentence
She graduated from the New York Medical College in 1870.

Third Sentence
Early engineers built this temple and library using a measurement system based on the earth's dimensions.

••SCIENCE STORY••

First Sentence
The Great Pyramid of Giza in Egypt was built from 2,500,000 blocks weighing between 2 and 70 tons.

Second Sentence
One third of the crops that are economically important in the U.S. today were cultivated by American Indians, including corn, cotton, potatoes, and beans.

Third Sentence
As a crew member, he conducted experiments with monocrystals and semi-conductors.

••SCIENCE STORY••

First Sentence
The first African American woman to become a medical doctor in the United States was Susan Maria Smith McKinnery Steward (1848-1918).

Second Sentence
Its corners were positioned to mark north, south, east, and west.

Third Sentence
An accomplished laser physicist, he collaborated in developing the spin-flip tunable laser.

••SCIENCE STORY••

First Sentence
Mayan cultures developed a complex calendar system which was used for over 2,000 years.

Second Sentence
He originated a method for long-term record keeping of insect behavior.

Third Sentence
He organized the first training center for African American nurses.

••SCIENCE STORY••

First Sentence
Written in 2600 BC, ancient Egyptian medical books explained the diagnosis and treatment of disease.

Second Sentence
In 1967, he invented the Diamond Window which made it possible for atomic scientists to manufacture new molecules.

Third Sentence
In his research, he found parallels between insect and human behavior.

••SCIENCE STORY••

First Sentence
In the early 1900's, Williamina Fleming was an astronomer at the Harvard Observatory.

Second Sentence
Their 365 day year consisted of 18 months of 20 days and 1 month of 5 days.

Third Sentence
Their calendars plotted solar eclipses and the movement of the planet Venus.

••SCIENCE STORY••

First Sentence
Daniel Hale Williams was the first surgeon to successfully open the chest cavity to perform surgery.

Second Sentence
She analyzed and classified the various types of radiation coming from stars.

Third Sentence
In addition to the Manhattan Project, he worked on the production of synthetic blood.

••SCIENCE STORY••

First Sentence
Charles Henry Turner was an animal behaviorist specializing in social insects, like bees.

Second Sentence
Both men and women learned to set broken bones, vaccinate against disease, perform surgery and treat everyday ailments.

Third Sentence
She became the first woman honored with an appointment as a curator at the Harvard Observatory.

••SCIENCE STORY••

First Sentence
Lloyd Albert Quarterman was one of 6 African American nuclear scientists working with Albert Einstein on the Manhattan Project.

Second Sentence
He helped establish Providence Hospital in Chicago, the first hospital to permit African American doctors to operate.

Third Sentence
Even in ancient times, people studied anatomy, dermatology, opthamology and dentistry.

Who's in Your Tree?

Age:
5-13
Participants:
Group, Family, Pair

Why

To stimulate thinking about school, work and life choices.

What

Every family is different. A family tree is one way to illustrate the uniqueness of your family. More than just a chart, it may show patterns, answer questions and hold surprises. It gives you a chance to look into family history and make predictions about the future. An alternative to making a family tree is to make a tree outlining the relationships in your neighborhood, church, school or community.

Making a family tree and researching the careers of family members is a fun way for children to explore their own interests and options for the future. Parents and other adults can demonstrate the connection between education and career choices by sharing stories about their own personal experiences.

How

Make a family tree.

- Cut down one side of the paper grocery bag, and then cut away the bottom. Flatten it into a large sheet. This becomes the background for your family tree.

- Cut out paper squares and triangles with 2 inch (5 centimeter) sides. Prepare at least 15 of each shape.

- Write the names of the children in your family on the paper shapes—use squares for males and triangles for females. Draw a key on the chart to show that ■= male and ▲= female.

- You may not know everyone who belongs in your family tree. When you're not sure about a person's name or family relationship, put a question mark on the shape. You may be able to fill it in later.

- Along the paper's bottom edge, arrange the children in your family in a horizontal line.

- Place parents directly above the children. In blended families, you may need to add additional adults or children.

- Add the parents' brothers and sisters (aunts, uncles) next to the

Supplies

- *paper grocery or shopping bag*
- *scissors*
- *recycled paper, with one clean side*
- *ruler*
- *pen or pencil*
- *transparent tape or glue*
- *mug*
- *dinner plate*
- *large bowl*

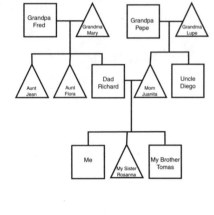

parents. Under the aunts and uncles add their children (cousins).

- Add grandparents on the next line above the parents. Continue writing names on each shape you add. You may have to adjust the shapes as you go so that they all fit on the paper.

- Continue adding shapes until you run out of people or space. Tape or glue the shapes in place. Use more paper if necessary.

- Connect the shapes as shown in the drawing.

- Once your tree is complete, make notes about the interests, education or careers of family members. Explore and discuss the following questions about your family.
  What types of work are represented—business, technical, medical, homemaker, farming, the arts, education, clergy?
  What patterns do you see?
  How many years did people go to school?
  Do any professions in your family tree occur more than once?
  Does anyone have more than one occupation?

Community Circles

Brainstorm your community career contacts.

- Turn the chart over or get a new piece of paper.

- Trace a mug, a dinner plate, and a large bowl, each over the other, to make three concentric circles.

- Put your family's name in the center circle.

- In the next ring, list the names and occupations of the workers with whom your family interacts on a daily and weekly basis. This list may include friends, teachers, co-workers, bus drivers, grocery store clerks, nurses, or repair people, etc.

- In the outside ring, list the occupations that provide service to all your friends and family. The list may include anyone from accountants to zookeepers. Check your community or family phone book to jog your memory.

- Count the number of occupations you've listed in each circle.

- What occupations would you like to add? What workers could help your family? Who would you like to meet? Are there any jobs in the circles that you would like to have? Write these thoughts around the outside of the circles.

Double or Divide

Age:
5-13
Participants:
Group, Family, Pair

Why

To stimulate discussions about life choices and options.

What

Keeping a journal or diary is one way to record daily life. Written in your own words, journal entries may describe your activities, thoughts or interactions with other people. Over time, a journal becomes a calendar of your life that's sometimes secret and always personal.

Adults often feel that time is flying. For children, time never seems to move fast enough. In this activity, adults can relive the past, while children creatively explore their future in words and pictures.

How

- Follow the directions for making a journal (see Chapter 4, *Making and Using a Science Journal*, page 81). Add blank paper to use as journal pages or collect a stack of paper for each participant.

- To begin, children multiply their age by 2. Adults divide their age by 2. Use a calculator if necessary. Make a chart to keep track of everyone's new age. For example:

Children: Multiply age by 2				Adults: Divide age by 2			
current age	5	8	10	current age	24	28	36
first round age	10	16	20	first round age	12	14	18

- In your journal, using words or pictures, describe a day of your life at your new age.
- Trade journals or take turns reading them aloud.
- Now for round 2. This time adults divide and children multiply their new ages by 2. Record the results on the chart, then write another entry in your journal.

Supplies

- *paper or journal*
- *calculator (optional)*
- *pencil*

For example:

Children: Multiply age by 2				Adults: Divide age by 2			
current age	5	8	10	current age	24	28	36
first round	10	16	20	first round age	12	14	18
second round	20	32	40	second round	6	7	9

- Look for patterns in your family about your lives at different ages. Answer a few of the following questions.
  Who do you spend time with?
  How many hours are spent at school or work?
  Who has a family? Children? Pets? Neighbors? What are they like?
  How many hours are spent doing homework or housework?
  How many hours are spent helping others?
  How many hours are spent watching television or participating in sports or recreational activities?
  Where do you live? Work?
  Who earns money? What do they buy?

- Try a third round to look back or toward the future.

Next

- Have a conversation with your children about what their lives would be like in the year of their new age. What kinds of new technologies might be in place by then? What new scientific discoveries do they anticipate will occur that year? Encourage your children to describe what their homes look like. What would they see as they walk down the street?

Bridges

Age:
8-13
Participants:
Group, Family, Pair

Why

To discuss the connections between school studies and the future.

What

A bridge is a means of connection. Children and adults build all kinds of bridges between school and daily life, home and school, school and the community. There are also learning bridges between content and understanding, ideas and actions, or research and experiments.

This activity presents new ideas, information, and strategies for future science learning. Your past bridge building experience can help you link school studies to daily life using science and mathematics.

Supplies

- *index cards (20 or more)*
- *paper*
- *pencil*
- *felt pens, 2 different colors*
- *adding machine tape*
- *tape*

How

- Make 2 decks of index cards with at least 10 cards in each deck.

- Brainstorm a list of words that relate to **school studies** and write them on a piece of paper, using one of the pen colors.

    For example:

computers	studying	history
memorization	tests	vocabulary
experiments	models	numbers
reading	textbooks	communication
measurement	graphs	questions

- Copy one word onto each index card in one of the decks.

- Next, brainstorm a list of words that relate to **daily life** and write them down too, using the second pen color.

    For example:

television	culture	role models
jobs	shelter	tools
neighborhood	health care	food
money	entertainment	recreation
transportation	family	church

- Copy one word onto each index card in the second deck.

- Shuffle each deck to mix up the words. Be sure to keep the decks separate. Set the decks face down.

- Turn over the top card in each deck.

- The group task is to build a bridge between the two words using science or mathematics ideas, activities, issues or strategies. For example, if your words were "computer" and "television," one bridge might be "electronic technologies."

- Record the bridge idea on a strip of the adding machine tape, and then attach the words to each end with tape.

- Continue turning over cards and building bridges until you use all the cards.

- Look for patterns in the bridges between school and daily life.
  How are the bridges similar? How are they different?
  Which bridges use science-related ideas? Mathematics?
  Which bridges link school studies to home? To the community?

Charting the Future

Age:
8-13
Participants:
Group, Family, Pair

Why

To encourage students to study science and mathematics at all grade levels. To highlight careers that involve science and mathematics.

What

Becoming an astronaut and traveling through outer space may be a first grader's dream. High school students enrolled in physics and calculus courses may be preparing for university studies that include space sciences. The choices we make about careers are linked to preparation, training, and opportunity. Sorting through a range of occupations is a good way to start conversations with children about their interests, future schooling, and work.

How

- Make a large sheet from a paper bag by cutting down one side and removing the bottom.

- Draw 7 columns on the flattened bag. Label the columns:
  Not sure
  No high school diploma
  High school diploma
  High school diploma + training
  College degree (4 years)
  Masters degree (College degree + 2 years)
  Ph.D. (College degree + 4 years)

- Draw a line under the column headings.

- Take turns choosing occupations from the *Science at Work* list on pages 62-63. Use the dictionary to check the meanings of occupations you don't recognize.

- Write the occupation under the heading that describes the education required. If you're not sure, write it in the "Not sure" column.

- There are other ways to code the occupations on your list:
  Underline jobs that may fit in more than one column.
  Add a # after occupations that are mathematics-based.
  Put a ★ after occupations that are science-based.
  Write the names of people you know after their occupation.

Supplies

- *large paper grocery bag*
- *scissors*
- *felt pen*
- *dictionary*
- *paper*
- *pencils*
- *weekly TV guide*

- After you've filled in the chart, each participant should secretly write on a separate paper the 3 occupations they are most interested in.

- Take turns trying to guess the choices others made. Continue until everyone has had a chance to participate.

- Have everyone put their initials on the chart next to the 3 occupations they chose.

- Review a weekly television guide to find out which occupations are portrayed on television. Add a ■ after each one on the chart.

- Add a key to the corner of your chart to describe what the following represent: underline, #, ★, initials, ■.

Next

- Check the local yellow pages to find jobs in your area to add to the *Science at Work* list.

- Find out more about the jobs in the "Not sure" column from resources at school, the library, at work or on the Web.

  - This activity may prompt you to seek more career information. Talk with librarians, school administrators or counselors, classroom teachers, friends, and mentors about special programs and courses, student employment, college admissions, training opportunities, selection tests, and financial assistance.

Science at Work: Occupation List

This list of occupations provides a starting place for learning about careers or finding people who use science in their work. Looking in your local telephone yellow pages will help you locate the workers in your community.

A
academic counselor
acoustical engineer
aerial surveyor
agronomist
anaesthesiologist
animal attendant
arborist
archaeologist
architect
astronaut
astrophysicist
audio engineer
audiologist
auto mechanic

B
bacteriologist
beekeeper
biochemist
biomathematician
blacksmith
boat builder
bookkeeper
botanist
building contractor

C
cabinet maker
cartographer
chemical salesperson
chemist
city planner
civil engineer
computer programmer
consumer researcher
coroner
curator
cytologist

D
dental hygenist
dentist
dietician
drafter
druggist
dry cleaner

E
ecologist
electrician
electronic technician
electroplater
exterminator

F
farmer
film developer
fish hatchery operator
florist
food inspector
forester

G
game warden
gardener
geneticist
geologist
geophysical surveyor
grain inspector

H
heating contractor
helicopter pilot
heavy equip operator
histopathologist
home economist
horticulturist
hydrologist

I
illustrator, medical
industrial hygienist
instrument maker
inventor
irrigation consultant

J
jeweler
journalist, science

L
laboratory technician
land-use planner
landscaper
lithographer
livestock dealer
locksmith

M
marine biologist
mason
mathematician
mechanical engineer
medical anthropologist
medical technician
metal fabricator
metallurgist

meteorologist
midwife
millwright
mineralogist
museum educator
mycologist

N
naturalist
navigator
nuclear medicine technician
nurseryman
nurse
nutritionist

O
occupational therapist
oceanographer
opthamologist
optician
orthodontist
organic grower

P
painter
paleontologist
paramedic
park superintendent
patent lawyer
photographer
physician
physicist
pilot
planetarium operator
plumber
power plant operator
printer
prosthetist
public health worker

Q
quality control tester

R
radiation health specialist
radio technician
rancher
respiratory therapist

S
safety officer
school teacher
seismologist
sewage treatment worker
soil scientist
solar energy installer
statistician
steam fitter
steel fabricator
surgeon
surveyor

T
technical salesperson
technical writer/editor
telecommunications technician
telescope operator
television producer
textile technican
tile layer
tool and die makers
toxicologist

U
upholsterer
undertaker
urban planner
utility consultant

V
viticulturist
veterinarian

W
water analyzer
water works supervisor
weather forecaster
welder
wildlife rehabilitator
woodworker
word processor

X
x-ray technician

Z
zoo keeper
zoologist

Meeting Career Role Models

Age:
5-13
Participants:
Group, Family, Pair

Why

To meet people who use science and mathematics in their work. To learn about the benefits and requirements for various careers.

What

A career role model is a member of the workforce who is interested in sharing the excitement and challenges of their work with others. Meeting career role models is one way for children to discover that work in the sciences is rewarding and realistic for them. Career role models demonstrate the connection between school and work. The diversity of the workforce should be reflected in the role models you recruit for this activity. Invite women, physically challenged individuals, and people from diverse ethnic and racial backgrounds who work in science, mathematics and technology-based fields.

How

Contacting career role models

- Review the *Finding Science: People and Places* list on pages 67-68 for ideas about where to look for a career role model in your community.

- Arrange a meeting or telephone conversation to invite the career role model to your class. Explain that this is an opportunity to inspire students and raise their career awareness. Make it clear that FAMILY SCIENCE is a volunteer activity.

- Mail a letter to your guest confirming the date, time, and location of the class. Include other information such as the expected number of participants, age or grade level of the students, an activity overview, and a contact name and phone number. Attach the list of *Frequently Asked Career Questions* (see page 69). An employer may require a written request from you in order to release an employee from work or to document his/her community service.

- Try the following activities with your career guest: *Question Marks* (page 70), *Who Is Telling The Truth* (page 72), *Tool Clues* (page 74).

Supplies

- *telephone book*
- *recruitment letter*
- *thank-you card*

Sample Career Role Model Letter

Date
Name
Address

Thank you for agreeing to participate in our FAMILY SCIENCE event. Our goal is to increase the participation of all students in science studies and to help them see how important science and math can be at work. Your presentation will help stimulate the students' interest in careers, show links between schooling and future jobs, and demonstrate the relevancy of science and mathematics to our lives.

Please check the information below to confirm the specifics of your visit:

Date, Day, Time
Number of Adults and Children Participating
Location, Room Number
Directions, Parking, and Other Considerations
Supplies, Materials or Equipment Requested
Contact Person and Phone Number

During FAMILY SCIENCE, parents and children work together to build their skills and find enjoyment in science learning. The setting is informal, so you do not need to prepare a formal presentation or lecture. A description of the career activity, the program goals, and a list of frequently asked questions is included for your review. After the activity is finished, there will be about fifteen minutes for comments and questions. A class leader will moderate the activity and the question period.

Thank you again for including FAMILY SCIENCE in your schedule. We hope you find this experience rewarding.

Sincerely,

FAMILY SCIENCE Team Members

Preparing for the visit

- The career guest should know what to expect during their visit. Explain that FAMILY SCIENCE events are informal, relaxed and friendly. Let them know the interests of participating families. Encourage brief, nontechnical comments during their presentation. If they have specific uniforms, tools or equipment that they use at work, encourage them to bring them along to show the class.

- Announce to the families in advance when a career guest will be attending. This provides an opportunity for families to plan their attendance, prepare questions or invite other family members. For some activities, the guest's identity is a mystery until after his/her presentation.

Presenting the career activity

- Arrange for someone to meet the guest when he/she first arrives. Offer the guest refreshments, introduce him/her to key people and show him/her where the presentation will take place.

- Distribute paper and pencils for writing questions and notes.

- A moderator should introduce the guest and explain the activity to the group. Announce any time limits.

- Check that everyone can hear, and be heard, during the presentation.

- When the activity and question period is over, have the moderator thank the guest in front of the group.

- A follow-up discussion may include requests for specific information, personal comments, or effective questioning strategies.

- Circulate a thank-you card for parents and children to sign. There is a copy-ready thank-you card on page 188.

- In some cases, a formal letter acknowledging the time commitment, community involvement and impact on families should be sent to the career guest with a copy sent to his/her employer.

- Start a list of career role models who live in your community. Include useful information, such as: name, address, occupation, employer and phone, contact person, visit date, activity, location, and size of the class. Additional information may include: the date the thank-you card was mailed, workplace acknowledgement, management problems, personal preferences, honorarium or gift, suggestions, or a list of tools used in their work.

Next

- Plan a tour by the career guest of his/her workplace.

- At the school or community center, display a scrapbook of comments, clippings, questions, and photos about career visitors.

- Plan a panel discussion of only non-traditional workers, for example, women who are university science professors or men who are nurses.

Finding Science: People and Places

Start with family, friends, co-workers, and neighbors, then just look around...

Community Locations

airport	hospital
aquarium	marine center
auto service	museum
botanical garden	music center
cultural center	movie theater
energy facility	nature center
environmental park	nursery
fire station	pet and hobby shop
fish hatchery	planetarium
grocery store	school
harbor or port	water treatment facility
health clinic	wildlife rehabilitation site
historic center	zoo

Community Service Agencies

agricultural extension	environmental quality	rural services
air quality control	fire department	soil conservation
animal and plant health	food and drug agency	speech & hearing clinic
animal shelter	forest management	transportation services
aviation safety	geological survey	weather services
blood bank	hazardous materials agency	wetlands management
bureau of labor	military services and facilities	wildlife enhancement
city planning and development	nuclear regulation	
community health services	nutrition services	
disabilities commission	occupational health	
disease control	park services	
emergency services	police department	
energy management	recycling center	

Workplaces

accounting office

architectural firm

art studio

broadcasting station

computer center

construction site

dairy

electrician shop

engineering office

factory

farm

food processing plant

foundry

industrial park

laboratory

locksmith shop

maintenance/repair shop

manufacturing shop

metal shop

military facility

mine

orchard

photography studio

plumbing company

power or mechanical plant

print shop

research facility

restaurant

telecommunications center

Educational Facilities

admissions offices

agricultural extension programs

apprenticeship programs

career planning services

community colleges

computer schools

federal training programs

high schools

industrial training programs

licensing boards

job training programs

medical or dental schools

mentorship programs

specialty training schools

universities

Community Networks

business associations

community service representatives

computer network groups

conservancy groups

churches

cultural organizations

disability services

education associations

emergency services

wildlife protection groups

fraternities and sororities

granges

hobbyist clubs

labor unions

minority organizations

scientific societies

service groups

volunteer services

Frequently Asked Career Questions

What is it like to be a _____?

Describe a typical day at your job.

How do you use science or mathematics in your work?

How does your work relate to our daily lives?

How much schooling is required for your job? Is it expensive?

What advice would you give to someone entering your field?

What do you do when you're not at work? Hobbies? Favorite books or TV shows? Sports? Housekeeping? Family?

Where, when and how do you work? Do you travel? Hours? Clothing?

When you were 12 years old, what job did you think you'd have as an adult?

If you could change one thing about your job, what would it be?

What did you learn in elementary school that is still useful now?

What did you do for fun as a child that improved your science and mathematics skills?

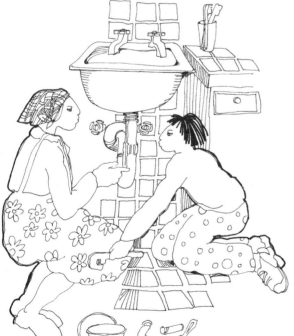

What people were instrumental in your pursuit of math and science? In what ways did they influence you?

Describe a problem you have solved or are trying to solve at work.

What do you like about your job? What has been your biggest challenge?

How does your job reward you? Opportunities? Salary range? Satisfaction?

When you were young did you like school?

What do the other people you work with do?

What tools do you use at work?

How do you learn new things about your work? Do you go to school or are you trained on the job?

What do you want to do in the future?

Question Marks

Why

To discover nontraditional jobs and workers.
To develop work values by learning what others feel about their work.

What

Guest speakers for a FAMILY SCIENCE event can discuss aspects of their particular careers, including what they perceive to be the advantages and disadvantages, salary ranges and necessary training and education. They may share their own experiences with school math or science and informal learning opportunities they had as a child. Their input will illustrate the relevance of science in our everyday life and the excitement of using science in a career.

How

In this activity, families will try to discover the occupation of a career guest by asking yes and no questions.

- Invite a career guest to visit your class. Review the section on *Meeting Career Role Models* (starting on page 64) for ideas.

- Select one person to moderate the activity.

- Draw a large question mark on each index card.

- Make a large chart with 2 columns. Write "families" on one side and the name of the career guest on the other side.

- Hang the 20 question marks on the "families" side of the chart.

- Allow time for families to think of a few questions that can be answered with yes or no responses. Encourage families to ask questions that will:
  eliminate possibilities
  provide new information
  lead to more questions
  identify skills or a work environment
  build on information you already know

- Have families take turns asking questions. If the answer is yes, the same family asks another question. If the answer is no, move a question mark to the guest's side of the chart, and the next family may ask a question.

Supplies

- *felt pen*
- *20 index cards*
- *large piece of paper or chalkboard and chalk*
- *tape*
- *thank-you card*

- Continue until all the question marks are moved or the occupation is discovered.

- Next, ask the guest to explain his/her job and answers further questions. Discussion topics may include job preparation, challenges, and the support he/she received for studies and work.

- Be sure to send a thank-you card to your career guest.

Next

- Career role models can schedule a follow-up visit to teach an activity related to their work or to share journals, photographs, books or tools.

- Individual students or family groups may arrange to visit the career guest at his/her work site.

- Students may invite the career guest for a classroom visit or present a homework report on his/her presentation.

Who is Telling the Truth?

Supplies
- *3 index cards*
- *scrap paper*
- *pencils*
- *3 thank-you cards*

Why

To explore the use of mathematics and science in many different occupations.

What

Knowledge of science and mathematics is important to all types of work, even in those occupations that are not based in science or mathematics. Parents and other adults can help children identify examples of mathematics and science being applied in the workplace.

How

- Invite 3 career guests to a FAMILY SCIENCE event. Look for people who work in nontraditional, service, technical or professional jobs that apply mathematics and science to their work. (Refer to *Meeting Career Role Models* on page 64 for ideas.)

- Select one job as a focus. All 3 guests will pretend they have the same job.

- The task is for each group to determine who is the "real" worker in the chosen occupation. The "real" worker must tell the truth; the other 2 guests can bluff or make up answers.

- Divide into family groups or small groups of 3-5 people.

- Seat the 3 panel members in view of all the participants. Fold each index card in half and label each one with a "1," "2," or "3." Put a numbered card in front of each guest.

- Introduce each guest and the selected occupation. For example, "Who is the real plumber, 1, 2 or 3 ?" "Who is the real nutritionist?" "Who is the real firefighter?"

- Groups may ask each guest one question that can be answered with a yes or no response. For example, "Guest Number One, do you use a computer daily?"

- At the end of the questioning period, each group writes its guess on a sheet of paper. Taking turns, groups display their vote and explain their choice.

- After the voting is complete, identify the "real" career guest.

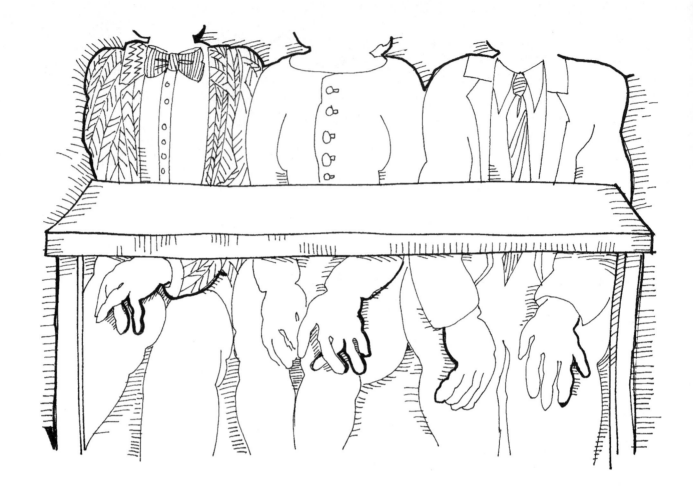

- The "imposter" career guests introduce themselves and describe their real occupations.

- The panel answers questions from the groups.

- Small group discussions may include the process they used to decide on their vote, characteristics common to all 3 guests, and skills required in each job.

- Be sure to send a thank-you card to each guest.

Next

- Encourage families to exchange pre-addressed envelopes with a career guest. They can then correspond with the guest, asking questions about his/her job, responding to the daily news, sharing ideas and describing stories of a typical day at school or work. (Be sure to get the okay from career guests before suggesting this activity.)

Tool Clues

Why

To demonstrate the connection between work and skills.
To become familiar with occupations through the tools workers use.

What

Asking questions about various careers and noting how your interests may relate to them is a good idea. How much math do you need to know? What science experiences are the best to have? What skills are needed? Which is the best school for a particular career? What careers have the most opportunity? The more questions you ask, the better prepared you will be when making choices in the future.

How

Groups try to determine a career guest's occupation using work tools as clues.

- Invite a career guest to visit your class. Review *Meeting Career Role Models* on page 64 for ideas.

- Ask the career guest to bring one work tool for each participating group. The tools don't need to be expensive or complex. For example, clipboards, tool pouches, computer disks, a red pencil or a flashlight might be tools brought by an engineer.

- Select one person to moderate the activity.

- Hide one tool in each bag along with paper and a pencil. Distribute one tool bag clue to each family group.

- Each group should quietly explore its clue, being careful to keep it hidden in the bag. Groups should then prepare one question to ask the career guest. The question should help the group learn more about how the tool is used in the guest's work.

- With careful wording, questions can be asked so that a group's tool clue remains a mystery to the rest of the group.

- When all the groups have asked one question, they write their guess about the guest's occupation on paper.

- The moderator collects the tools and written guesses.

Supplies

- *large paper grocery bags*
- *paper*
- *pencils*
- *thank-you card*

- The career guest reads the guesses, reveals his/her occupation, and identifies each tool and how it is used in their daily work.

- A question and answer session follows.

- Be sure to send a thank-you card to your guest after the activity.

Next

- Borrow a set of tools that belong to a geologist, mechanical engineer, farmer, or seamstress. Display the tool set and allow families to guess what occupation would use the set of tools. Reveal the tool owner at the end of the class.

- Ask participants to demonstrate the tools they use for work or recreation. Examples may include: a glass cutter used for stained glass work or home construction; a siphon used when boating or for automotive repair; a calculator used to play board games or help with small business accounting.

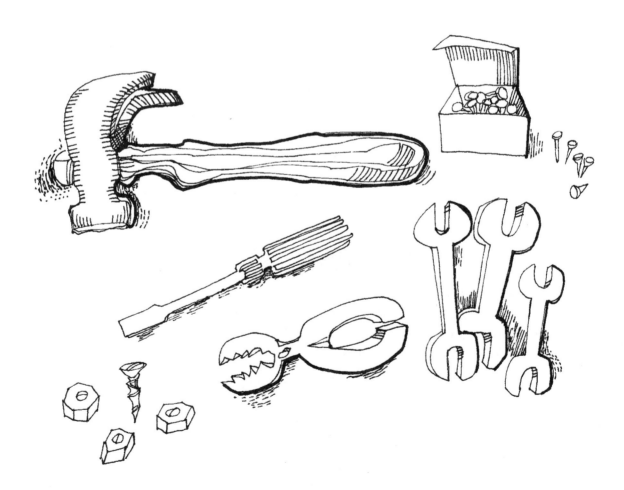

Family Science Field Trips

Age:
5-13
Participants:
Group, Family, Pair

Why

To familiarize children with community resources and workplaces for science learning.

What

The place to start moving science from textbook study to active learning is right outside your door. Your own community can be a great laboratory for science learning. A science field trip could be a visit to a science and technology museum, an industry tour, a trip to a local planetarium, or an outing to the county fair. Visiting various job sites shows the relevancy of science to our daily lives and increases the number of options for family trips.

How

- Discuss places family members would like to visit as a science field trip. Look at the list below for ideas. You can also consult *Finding Science: People and Places* on pages 67-68.

public service announcements	advertisements
radio or television programs	local newspapers
city guides	telephone books
community newsletters	professional bulletins
teachers	other families
science books or films	school projects
career guests	historical societies
nature groups	universities
visitor information centers	professional groups

- Open up the map. Locate your street, then mark any field trip destinations you can find.

- Talk over your ideas. Use the telephone book to gather additional information. Check the hours of operation, costs, route and other details to help focus your choice.

- Get out the calendar. Pick a day and time for a science field trip. You may want to combine it with a routine or planned trip.

- Mark the field trip on your calendar. Post a list of things family members need to do before the trip.

Supplies

- *local map*
- *pencil*
- *telephone book*
- *time schedules for transportation and facility*
- *calendar*

- Talk over with your family what you would like to do when you reach your destination.

Activities To Consider

take a hike

schedule a tour

go behind the scenes

draw pictures

research information

write in your journal

collect samples

repair something

attend a meeting/presentation

watch an assembly process

listen to a lecture

go on a treasure hunt

take photographs

build something

use a computer

take turns reading aloud

test materials

follow a map to key points

pretend you work there

collect data

follow a worker

take a class or workshop

CHAPTER 4
USING THE LANGUAGE OF SCIENCE

Making and Using a Science Journal

Supplies

- *construction paper or lightweight cardboard*
- *scissors*
- *hole punch*
- *3-hole paper*
- *one type of fastener (string, ribbon, yarn, garbage bag ties, notebook rings, etc.)*
- *ruler*
- *pencils*
- *tape*

Why

To encourage writing down science-related ideas, observations and experiences.

What

Journal writing helps put language skills and science together. Writing provides an opportunity to reflect, analyze and record observations. It can even motivate us to explore our curiosity further. Writing is one way to find out what we know, understand or feel about a topic. In a science journal you can collect questions, record events, gather information, or collect samples of news articles. Every now and then review your journal with your family to get ideas for future trips, activities or experiments.

How

This activity guides you through making and using a science journal.

- Begin by making a cover for your journal. Use 2 sheets of construction paper or thin cardboard for the cover.
- Cut down the cover pages to the same size as your 3-hole paper.
- Place a piece of 3-hole paper on top of your cover pages to use as a guide. Mark the 3 holes with a pen, and punch out the holes with a hole punch.
- Open the cover. Place a stack of paper inside, lining up the holes.
- Close the cover. Thread the fasteners through the front cover, paper stack and back cover for all 3 holes.
- Illustrate and label the cover. Draw pictures, make a collage or simply add color. Use your imagination!
- Use the journal to record words and drawings about science experiences. Consider adding graph paper, maps, charts, clippings, or diagrams to your journal to enhance your entries.
- Using differently sized paper, construct journals for special projects, school reports or family trips.

Science Journal Writing Ideas

Some of the activities in this FAMILY SCIENCE book may instruct you to write ideas or results in a journal. Here are some other ideas to get you started on journal writing.

- How would you improve the planet? What would you like to invent? What famous scientist would you like to meet? What do you like or dislike about science? What makes you curious?

- Describe all the living things you can see from one window in your home. Give your written description to someone else and see if they can figure out which window you were looking out.

- Write about a problem you solved at school or home this week.

- Keep a record of all the steps you followed to do an experiment.

- Clip and read a science newspaper article. Write down what you thought about the article.

- Observe the moon every day for a month. Note the date, time, and its location in the sky. After each observation, draw a picture in your journal.

- Take something apart—an orange, retractable ballpoint pen, tea bag—and describe it in your journal. Draw pictures, diagram the parts, or write instructions on how to put it back together.

Did you know..?

Writing down your science ideas could someday lead to an important discovery or serve as a reference to help others. In 1552, an Aztec physician named Marinus de la Cruz wrote down his ideas and compiled them into the Badianus Manuscript, a guide to the herbal plants used to heal the Aztec people.

Natural Guesses

Supplies

- *paper*
- *felt pens*
- *tape*
- *pencils*
- *calculators*
- *resource materials (books, magazines, encyclopedias, etc.)*

Why

To promote curiosity about the natural world.
To make estimates and calculations.
To compare prior knowledge and research new information.

What

Our appreciation of living things increases when we learn about their unique qualities. You may find that you have something in common with a plant that grows in soil or an animal that flies at night. Our curiosity is aroused by new information. In this activity, try making some guesses about the world around you.

How

- Copy one question onto a sheet of paper for each person or pair from the following list. You may need to make multiple copies of some questions.

Questions

1. How long do brown bats live?
2. How many feathers does a bald eagle have?
3. What percent of a potato is water?
4. How many quills does the common North American porcupine have?
5. How many times does a mosquito move its wings in a second?
6. Your heart is the size of your fist and weighs about a pound (half a kilogram). How much does a giraffe's heart weigh?
7. How old is the oldest living tree?
8. How many different species of spiders live on the earth?
9. There are tiny holes or pores in egg shells. How many pores are in a chicken's egg shell?
10. How many teeth does an adult opossum have?

- Tape a question to each person's back, so he/she cannot see it.

- Instruct the group to move about the room offering answers to the questions. Tell participants not to reveal the question to the person wearing it.

- Each person writes down 5 answers to his/her question given by other people.

- After collecting 5 answers, each person should calculate the average by adding the 5 answers, then dividing the total by 5. Make calculators available.

- Each person removes his/her question. Take turns reading each question out loud.

- Invite everyone with the same question to announce their average answer. The group decides whether the average answer is high, low, or about right. If reference materials are available, allow time for each person to research an answer to their question. Use library or Internet resources. Then reassemble the group to compare the previous estimates and averages with the researched information. Have individuals who's guesses were the closest to the researched answers share how they arrived at their answers. The group leader can then reveal the answers provided below and share additional reference information.

- Keep a list of any new questions asked.

Next

- Questions can be posted on charts or graphs on which participants write their guesses. Later, the actual answers and reference information can be attached to the charts.

Answers and Information

1. **20 or more years**–Bats live in all 50 states, and they are found almost everywhere in the world. The brown bat is the most common bat in North America. The smallest bats are the size of a bee, and the largest have more than a 4 foot wing spread. Bats play an important role in nature by eating millions of moths, flies and other insects and helping to pollinate many kinds of plants.

2. **About 7,180**–Birds don't usually have their feathers counted, but the number can range from 940 to 25,000 depending on the size of the bird. When feathers are broken or worn out, birds often produce new feathers to replace the old ones. The loss of feathers is called molting. Once a year, most birds molt all their feathers; not all at once, but gradually. Some birds molt twice a year. A bald eagle can be up to 7 years old before it has its full adult plumage with a pure white head and tail.

3. **78%-80%**–About 15% of a potato is starch, 2% protein, 1% minerals, and 0.1% fat. Potatoes provide the world with 6,000,000 metric tons of protein.

4. **About 36,000**–A porcupine's quills are located on its head, cheeks, legs, feet and tail. The quills are about 4 inches (10 centimeters) long. There are about 240 quills per square inch on an adult porcupine. Below the tip of each quill are 1,000 microscopic barbs. The quills provide protection for the porcupine, but porcupines cannot shoot their quills.

5. **Up to 600 times per second**–The hum you hear when a mosquito goes by is a clue to how fast its wings are moving. By comparison, the wingbeats for a housefly are 200 beats per second, a bee 190 per second, a dragonfly 28 per second, and a butterfly 8-12 per second.

6. **About 25 pounds (11 kilograms)**–The tallest of all mammals, a giraffe may reach a height of 18 feet (5.5 meters). The giraffe's heart has to be large in order to pump blood up its long neck to the head. Its long neck and tongue, which can extend up to 10 inches (46 centimeters), allows it to find food in places few other animals can reach.

7. **Between 4,600 to 4,900 years old**–The oldest living trees are believed to be bristlecone pines (*Pinus aristata*), which grow in the Western U.S. Bristlecone pines rarely grow taller than 35 feet (10.7 meters).

8. **More than 40,000**–Spiders are divided into 7 groups and many families. As many as 14,000 spiders may live on one acre of woodland in a given state.

9. **About 7,000**–When an egg is heated, the air inside the shell expands, and you can see the air escaping through the holes when the water boils. The pores are small enough to keep harmful bacteria from getting into the egg, but large enough to let the heated air out.

10. **50**–How many teeth do you have? Opossums use their teeth to eat fruit, insects, small vertebrates and garbage. The opossum is the only marsupial living outside of Australia. Marsupials are mammals that carry their young in a frontal pouch until fully developed. It is commonly thought that opossums play dead when frightened; however, they only become temporarily paralyzed from their fear. Therefore, the opossum is not playing dead but is suffering from shock.

Question Quilt

Supplies

- *a square yard of paper*
- *transparent tape*
- *construction paper or other colored paper*
- *scissors*
- *felt pen*
- *yard stick*
- *reference materials, resources*

Why

To develop an interest in science questions relevant to daily life.
To use a variety of resources to answer questions.

What

We all have things we wonder about. Why does the bathroom mirror steam up? What causes static cling? Why is the sky blue? You may find answers by making an observation, testing an idea, talking with your grandmother or checking a reference book. Sometimes no one knows the answer or there may be multiple answers. In this activity, you can collect and organize your everyday questions into a Question Quilt.

How

- To start a group Question Quilt, use one large sheet of paper or smaller sheets taped together to make a square yard. This paper will be the answer sheet.

- Cut 36, 6 by 6 inch (15 by 15 centimeters) squares from colored paper. These will be the quilt blocks.

- On the large answer sheet draw 6 rows and 6 columns of squares. Place 1 colored quilt block on top of each 6 by 6 inch square. Tape the top edge of each quilt block to the answer sheet. The blocks act as flaps that can be lifted over each square.

- Write a question on the front of one block, and then lift the block to write the answer in the square underneath. The flaps give everyone a chance to think about the questions before they read an answer.

- Hang a sign inviting other people to contribute to the Question Quilt in the following ways: draw a picture or diagram, add a related question, leave an answer to a question, or suggest a resource to help someone find the answer. If there is a question that interests you but you don't know the answer, research possible answers using books, magazines or the Internet. Read and enjoy the questions other people have.

- Magazine pictures, drawings, diagrams, or newspaper clippings may be added to illustrate questions or answers.

- Continue adding questions and answers until the group has filled the Question Quilt blocks.

Starter Questions and Answers

Where is the funny bone?

The funny bone is a place on the back of the elbow where the ulnar nerve passes close to the skin surface. A sharp impact at this place causes a strange tingling sensation in the arm.

Why do golfers use tees?

A golf tee raises the golf ball making it easier to hit without damaging the ground around it. George Grant, an African American inventor, received the patent for the golf tee in 1899.

Why does glass break into jagged pieces?

Most solids have crystalline structures, which means that the atoms or molecules are arranged in a repeating geometric pattern. Crystalline materials fracture along the geometric lines of the crystal. Glass is a combination of a solid and a liquid. Glass fractures in any direction, indicating that it is not made up of a geometric pattern of crystals.

How many gallons of sap does it take to produce 1 gallon of maple syrup?

35-45 gallons

How far can a flea jump?

A flea can broad jump about 15 inches (38 centimeters). Humans, using the same comparison, would be able to broad jump 700 feet (213 meters).

How does the soda get up the straw to my mouth?

When you use a straw, you create a tight seal between your mouth and the straw. The action of sipping lowers the air pressure inside the straw to a point slightly lower than the air pressure on the surface of the liquid, which pushes the liquid up the straw.

What is the earth's crust made of?

The most abundant elements are oxygen, silicon, aluminum, iron, calcium, sodium, potassium, and magnesium.

Why are cellophane packages hard to open?

Pulling at the cellophane spreads your force over a large area and causes stretching. If instead you start a tear, the stress is concentrated at a single point, and you do not have to pull very hard to continue the tear.

Why do onions make you cry?

Onion cells contain an oil that is released when you cut the onion, and the oil vapor enters your nose. The nerves inside your nose are connected to your eyes, and your eyes try to wash away the irritation with tears.

Why does a salty cracker taste sweet after you chew it for awhile?

Saliva mixes with food when you chew to help break it down before reaching your stomach. Chewing changes the cracker into the simple sugars that your body can use for energy, and you can taste this sugar while the cracker is in your mouth.

Next

The following list provides some starting places for finding answers to your questions.

- Check out books from a school or community library

- Ask people you know

- Look in a dictionary or encyclopedia

- Use the World Wide Web or send an e-mail on the Internet

- Take a field trip

- Read the label or directions

- Arrange a meeting with a career role model

- Talk with other parents and children

- Call an information center listed in the phone book

- Follow-up with a science teacher at a local school or university

- Make observations

- Conduct an experiment

- Find someone who works in the field

- Write to a research facility

- Visit an exhibit at a science center or museum

Evidence, Please

Supplies

- *paper, a variety of types*
- *paper clips*
- *clear plastic cups*
- *small flashlight*
- *small portable mirror*
- *plastic soda straw*
- *sheet of aluminum foil*
- *tape*
- *balloons*
- *spoons*
- *rubber bands*
- *pencil*
- *string*
- *ruler*
- *resealable sandwich bags*

Why

To test ideas and offer explanations for findings.

What

Scientists ask questions about the world around them and search for evidence to confirm their ideas. Evidence can support some things, but it may require ongoing investigation before a conclusion is reached. The challenge of this activity is to find evidence that demonstrates a science idea or concept for others using household items.

How

- Divide into teams. Collect one large set of supplies for the whole group. You may want to add other household materials to your supply list.

- Each team selects one of the topics on the *Evidence, Please List* to investigate using their collection of household materials (see page 90). For a challenge, one team can choose a topic for another team to investigate and demonstrate.

- Decide how much time you will have to investigate the selected topic, and prepare a demonstration of your evidence.

- Use the *Evidence, Please List* for ideas on what evidence to demonstrate. Practice your demonstration to be sure it shows the evidence you want.

- Each team presents their evidence on the selected topic.

- During the presentations, record other science ideas you discovered on the *Evidence, Please List*.

- Add answered and unanswered questions to a Question Quilt (see page 86 for a full description of this activity).

Evidence, Please List

Topic	Properties to demonstrate as evidence
Air	Air has weight and takes up space. Air can move objects. Air pressure is reduced by moving air.
Friction	Friction produces heat. Friction causes objects to resist movement. Friction can produce static electricity. Wheels reduce friction.
Water	Water can be absorbed. Some substances dissolve in water. Stirring shortens the dissolving time. Water pressure is not the same at all depths.
Shadows	A shadow is cast when light is blocked. One object can cast shadows of many different shapes. The distance between the object and the light source affects the size of the shadow.
Sound	Vibrating objects produce sound. Objects can be identified using sound. Sound can move through solid objects.
Human Beings	The senses help people identify objects, substances and events. Thumbs give humans a manual dexterity advantage. People adjust their center of gravity to remain balanced.
Reflection	Reflection is one way light changes direction. A reflection of a reflection can be viewed. Images reflected in a flat mirror are reversed. The location of an image in a mirror depends on the distance of the object from the mirror.
Light	Light travels in a straight line. Light can be reflected.
Structures	A hollow structure can be light and strong. The stronger the structure the more weight it can support. The shape of a structure affects the rigidity and strength of the structure.

Volley

Supplies

- *paper*
- *pens or pencils*

Why

To discuss science issues that invite personal opinions and may lead to decision making.
To distinguish between scientific evidence and personal opinion.

What

During discussions, people consider both positive and negative aspects of a subject. Discussions set the stage for expressing ideas and gaining insights. Communicating different points of view can help people find a compromise, change their perspective or encourage them to seek additional information.

In volleyball and tennis, a volley describes the return of the ball in play before it touches the ground. In this activity, you will volley with words instead of balls.

How

- Look for discussion topics in the newspaper, science magazines, on the World Wide Web, at school or at work. Try to find at least 8 different topics.

- Write a one sentence statement that relates to each topic on separate sheets of paper. There are topic and statement suggestions on the next page.

- Spread the statements face down on the table. To begin, one person randomly picks a statement and reads it aloud.

- To begin the volley, someone must immediately respond to the statement. Other group members should keep the volley going by joining in the discussion. The only person who doesn't respond is the one who reads the original statement.

- One person talks at a time. You may want to use a hand signal to let the group know you have something to say.

- After each person speaks, identify which parts of their response are based on scientific evidence and which are personal opinion.

- When the discussion stops, another person picks up a new statement sheet and begins another volley.

- After your group has completed a few rounds, discuss some of the following questions.

  What are the shared values in the group? What are some differences?

  What are the differences, if any, between scientific evidence and personal opinion?

  How would your group go about identifying options? Making decisions?

Volley Topics & Statement Suggestions

World Population

- The increasing world population puts a strain on our natural resources.
- Population control policies, like those in China, are controversial.
- Some groups believe that the world population is approaching the earth's carrying capacity.

Endangered Species

- Declaring a living thing an endangered species guarantees its survival.
- As the world's population increases, so will the number of endangered species.
- Saving endangered species is critical to our own survival.

Technology

- Computer, video and phone line networks improve communication.
- Advances in medical technology will eventually make it possible to live for 200 years.
- All technology is helpful in some way.

FAMILY SCIENCE

Crystal Packages

Supplies

- *copy of Crystal Packages Experiment*

- *scissors*

- *paper*

- *pencils*

- *plastic garbage bag*

- *bottle of water*

- *white paper towels*

- *magnifier*

- *white sugar*

- *brown sugar*

- *measuring spoons with metric measures*

- *4 twist ties*

- *4 plastic straws or craft sticks*

- *6 clear plastic cups, 6 oz. or larger*

- *watch with second hand*

- *powdered sugar*

- *KOOL-AID (with sugar already added)*

- *thermometer*

- *food color*

- *2 shallow dishes*

Why

To make measurements.
To observe and record changes during an experiment.

What

Sugar is a crystalline substance. Crystals are solids with atoms or molecules that link together in a repeating geometric pattern. When a sugar crystal comes in contact with water, some of the sugar molecules separate from each other and mix with the water. The sugar dissolves, creating a solution. A solution is a mixture in which one substance is dissolved in another. In this activity, you will perform an experiment with sugar crystals to see what happens when they are mixed with water.

How

- Make a photocopy of the *Crystal Packages Experiment* on page 95.

- The directions are not in order. Cut on the dotted lines to separate the 8 steps.

- Read each card so that everyone is familiar with the steps.

- Decide which step you will do 1st, 2nd, 3rd, continuing until all 8 of the cards are in order. You may want to number each step.

- This step-by-step experiment is like an investigation. There are opportunities for your family to ask questions and plan new experiments.

- When you have completed the *Crystal Packages Experiment*, make a photocopy of *Crystal Packages Continued* on page 96. Use the next 8 cards to continue experimenting.

Next

- Find a science experiment on the Web, or in a book. Take it apart! Write each step of the experiment on a card. Before you do the experiment, work with your family to put the steps in order.

- Challenge everyone in your family to find something in their daily life that relates to some part of the *Crystal Packages Experiment*.

- Make a booklet out of the Crystal Packages' steps, adding new pages as you try new experiments.

- Find a science pen pal. Write down a question you and your family had while you were working, and send it to your pen pal. Enclose a stamped, self-addressed envelope so that it will be easy to respond. Who could be your science pen pal? Here are some suggestions:

classroom teacher	friend or family member
research librarian	school science teacher
university instructor	research scientist
science news writer	science organization representative
college student	special interest group member
T.V. or radio personality	health care worker

Did you know..?

Norbert Rillieux (1806-1894) developed a process to refine white sugar. He applied his knowledge of steam engines to construct the Rillieux Vacuum Pan Process. This vacuum evaporation process revolutionized the sugar processing industry. Sugar is the number one food additive today. Other products, including glue, gelatin, soap and condensed milk, are also produced using his method.

Crystal Packages Experiment

Cut out along the dotted lines

- Cut a dry square paper towel into 4 equal sections.

- Place 1 teaspoon (5 milliliters) of white sugar in the center of a paper towel section.

- Do the same with a teaspoon of brown sugar in the center of another section.

- Describe the wet substances.

- Compare the dry and wet observations.

- Discuss the similarities and differences you observed.

- Observe the packages in the water for 3 minutes. Record your observations.

- Remove the packages from the water and observe the sugar crystals. Record your observations.

- To make a cover for your work area, cut open the side seams of a plastic trash bag.

- Wipe the table with a damp paper towel, and then spread the cover over the wet area.

- Collect the following:

2 sheets of paper	white sugar
pencil	brown sugar
plastic trash bag	measuring spoons
scissors	2 twist ties
bottle of water	2 straws or craft sticks
paper towels	2 clear cups
magnifier	watch w/second hand

- Write "questions or ideas" across the top of a sheet of paper or in your journal, and then record questions or ideas you have while you work.

- Bridge the top of the cups with a straw so that one package hangs inside each cup. Note how far down each package extends.

- Discuss what will happen to the crystal packages when they are in water.

- Remove the packages and pour enough water into the cups so that when the packages hang inside, they will be partially covered. Reinsert the packages.

- To make crystal packages, twist the corners of each paper towel section together. Hold them closed with twist ties.

- Use the ends of the twist tie to attach each package to the middle of a straw or craft stick.

- Use a magnifier to observe your sample of each sugar.

- Make a chart in your journal like the one below to record your observations.

Observations	dry	in water	wet
white sugar			
brown sugar			

Crystal Packages Continued

Cut out along the dotted lines

- Collect additional supplies:

  powdered sugar   2 straws or craft sticks

  KOOL-AID   2 twist ties

  4 clear cups   food color

  thermometer   2 shallow dishes

  paper

- Pour the sugar solution into a shallow dish. Place the dish in a warm or sunny location.

- The water will change into water vapor. This is evaporation. What will happen to the sugar when the water evaporates? Make a list of ideas.

- Mark the starting date on the calendar, and then check the sugar solution daily.

- After the water evaporates, observe what happened. Evaporation is one way to separate substances from solutions. Can you think of other ways to make this happen?

- Make packages for powdered sugar and KOOL-AID.

- List both on the observation chart.

Observations	dry	in water	wet
white sugar			
brown sugar			
powdered sugar			
KOOL-AID			

- Make 2 packages with the same type of sugar.
- Predict what will happen when you put 1 package in hot water and the other in cold. Record your prediction, and then try it.

Predictions	hot	cold
white sugar		
brown sugar		
Observations	hot	cold
white sugar		
brown sugar		

- Compare your predictions with your observations.

- Add 1 drop of food color to a cup of water. Observe what happens.

- Mix one teaspoon of each type of sugar in a cup half filled with water. Stir to form a solution.

- Discuss what would happen if you added a drop of food color to each of the sugar solutions.

- Add 1 drop to each sugar solution, and then observe what happens.

- Check the ingredients list on each package.

- Which of the ingredients can you observe when the substances are dry? In the water? Wet?

- Change how long the packages are in water.

- Make a chart in your journal to record results.

	white sugar	brown sugar
1 minute		
3 minutes		
5 minutes		
7 minutes		
10 minutes		

Our family wonders about:

_____

_____

_____

_____

_____

_____

Word Factory

Supplies

- *copies of the Word Factory cards*
- *pencil*
- *scissors*
- *index cards (optional)*
- *dictionary*
- *paper*
- *crayons or colored felt pens (optional)*

Why

To develop skills for recognizing and understanding science words.

What

Vocabulary can be a barrier to science learning, or it can help us. When we don't know the meaning of a word, it becomes more difficult to understand what we are reading or hearing. Yet, learning new words and meanings can complement hands-on science activities. Exploring words is both a language and a science skill. In this activity, you will creatively build words while learning the "real" meanings of science words.

How

- Make a deck of 24 *Word Factory* cards from the following two-sided patterns (see pages 99-104). Use a photocopier to make two-sided copies onto stiff or colored paper. Cut apart on the dotted lines. The words or word fragments may also be handwritten on the front and back of index cards.

- Familiarize yourself with the cards. One side of the card has the beginning of a word, a prefix. The other side of the card is the end of a word, a suffix. Each card makes a word when you combine the front and back.

- Try putting 2 cards together to make a new word. Figure out the meaning by reading the italicized words under the prefix and suffix.

- Turn the cards over to form another new word. Check the dictionary to see if the new word is commonly used.

- Divide into teams. Each team writes a sentence using one or more of the words built using *Word Factory* cards. Teams may also choose to draw pictures that help illustrate the new word.

- Trade sentences with another team. Try to figure out the meanings of the new words. Write your own definitions. For example:
  sentence   Magicians practice cryptokinesis.
  definition   Cryptokinesis means hidden movement.

- Take turns reading the sentences and definitions.

- Display your sentences (and pictures, if you have them) on the refrigerator.

re-	**-friger**	**-ator**
(over again)	(to make cold)	(that which does)

Next

- Add more prefix and suffix cards to the deck. For ideas, look in school science books, surf the Web, check newspapers or magazines, or add words you learn during a field trip.

Did you know..?

As a child, George Carruthers read science fiction books about space travel. He earned a B.S. in aeronautical engineering in 1961, an M.S. in nuclear engineering in 1962, and a Ph.D. in aeronautical and astronautical engineering in 1964. He invented the first camera used in outer space. His design, the Fari-Ultraviolet Camera Spectrograph, was installed on the moon by Apollo 16 astronauts. After doing this activity, take apart the name of his camera to learn what it does.

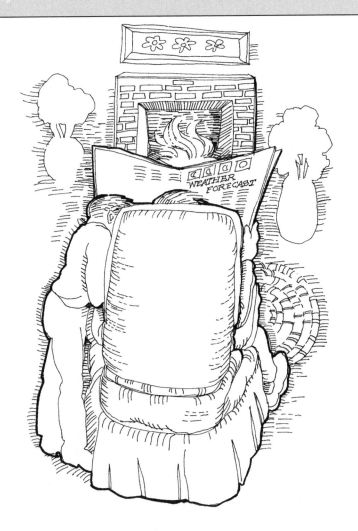

Word Factory–Set A: Front

hemo- *blood*	**petro-** *rock, stone*
tele- *far, distant*	**chromo-** *color*
bio- *life*	**thermo-** *heat*
micro- *very small*	**pachy-** *thick*

-philia

love of

-phone

device for listening

-oleum

oil

-some
-soma

body

-logy

study of

-meter

device for measuring

-scope

device for viewing

-derm

skin

Word Factory–Set B: Front

cosmo- *universe (world)*	**ecto-** *outside*
poly- *much, many*	**hydro-** *water*
geo- *earth*	**crypto-** *hidden*
photo- *light*	**zoo-** *animal*

-tron

instrument

-mer
-merous

part

-morph
-morphic

shaped like

-synthesis

place together

-plasm
-plasma

blood

fluid

-lysis

dissolve,
loosen

-lyze

dissolving,
loosening

-graph

something
that writes
or pictures

-gram

something
written down

-metry

measuring

Word Factory–Set C: Front

aero- *air, gas*	**ortho-** *straight, standard*
chloro- *green*	**cryo-** *cold, freezing*
macro- *large*	**heli-** *sun*
astro- *star*	**xeno-** *strange*

-nomy
knowledge of

-genesis
*origin,
formation,
evolution*

-phyll
leaf

-stat
stationary

-phage
eater

-phagous
eating

**-trope
-tropic
-tropism**
*turn, grow
toward or away*

-lith
stone

**-naut
-nautical**
navigate

Word Shuffle

Supplies

- *Word Factory cards, 6 sheets of 8 cards*
- *paper*
- *index cards (optional)*
- *felt pens*
- *scissors*
- *dictionary, one or more*
- *pencils*

Why

To identify science words and their meanings.

What

Paragraphs are made of sentences. Sentences are made of words. Many science words are made of prefixes and suffixes. Prefixes and suffixes are parts of words that define the words. By knowing the parts, we can learn to decipher scientific or technical words.

How

- Make one-sided copies of the *Word Factory* cards (see pages 99-104), and then cut them apart. You can also write the words on index cards to make a 48 card deck.

- Choose a dealer to give 5 cards to each player.

- Place the remaining cards on the table, face down. Turn over the top card and place it next to the deck. This is the discard pile.

- Take turns. Players may take the displayed card, one card from the deck, or the entire discard pile. At the end of their turn, they must place one card face up in the discard pile.

- Players look for pairs of cards that make real words by combining the prefix and suffix. Use the dictionary to check your words. If the words are not in the dictionary, they can still be used if the group agrees they make sense.

- Players may display their new word pairs on the table during their turn.

- Continue until one player uses all of his/her cards. That person deals for the next round.

- You may want to keep score with players earning 1 point for each word created, 2 points if the word is in the dictionary.

Next

- Deal 7 cards to each player. Use the dictionary at the end of the game to check for every real word.

FAMILY SCIENCE

Science Fictionary

Why

To discuss science words and meanings.
To communicate ideas in written language.

What

Students may learn as many new words in a science class as in a foreign language class. We often learn new words at the same time as we learn new information. Using a dictionary and talking with others is one way to take the mystery out of words. Even familiar words—such as matter, contact, or pole—have scientific meanings that are different from our everyday use.

How

Divide into groups of 2-5 players.

- Decide who will be the first player. He/she selects a word from the *Science Fictionary List* on pages 107-108, and then checks for the word in the dictionary.

- Next, he/she writes down the selected word for everyone to see.

- Each player writes a fictional definition for the word while the first player copies the scientific definition from the dictionary. You may work in teams to write definitions.

- The first player collects and shuffles all the definitions, and then reads the definitions aloud.

- Each player votes for the definition he/she thinks is the real one.

- The first player reveals the correct definition of the word.

- Continue taking turns until everyone has had a chance to pick a word, use the dictionary, and read the definitions.

Next

- Collect new words to add to the *Science Fictionary List.*

Supplies

- *copies of Science Fictionary List*
- *dictionary, larger than pocket version*
- *paper, the same size and color*
- *pencils*

Science Fictionary List

A antenna, aorta, aeronautics, ampere, apogee

B bicep, bivalve, bryophyte, burette, biped

C camouflage, conifer, carnivore, capacitor, cordate

D deciduous, dextrose, dormant, diatom

E emulsion, eddy, ekistics

F fauna, fulcrum

G geode, glottis, geyser

H hybrid, hygrometer, hyperbola, hectare

I ion, inertia, invertebrates, isotherm

J joule, jugular

K kilometer, keratin, kinematics

L lunar, legume, loess

M melanin, magma, meniscus, miscible

N nova, node, neap tide

O ozone, optics, ohm, ossify

P pupa, pollination, penumbra, perigee

Q quasar, quadrant, quark, quetzal

R   rheostat, remora, retina, rhizome

S   sepal, solenoid, sclerosis, stapes

T   tuber, thalamus, tropism, torque

U   uvula, umbel, umbra, ulna

V   vacuole, vertex, villus, viscosity, varve

W   watt, whey, whelk

X   xenon, xenophobe, xerophyte, xylem

Y   yttrium, yew, ytterbium

Z   zephyr, zenith, zoophyte

Details

Supplies

- *2 of each of the following: paper towel, rubber band, paper clip, toothpick, paper cup, or other household items*

- *medium size cardboard box*

- *scissors*

- *paper*

- *pencils or pens*

Why

To communicate using clear, precise language or pictures that represent objects.

What

Computer programming requires detailed language because computers perform detailed jobs. The speed, scale and precision of a computer exceeds what people can do, but the program that directs the computer's work is written by people.

In this activity, you'll use detailed language to communicate to another person about what you want to happen. The communication skills used are the same ones useful in recording observations, applying science terms, or interpreting technical language.

How

In this activity, use words or pictures to guide your partner to assemble objects in a particular way.

- Working with a partner, collect 2 of a number of identical objects.

- Divide the objects into 2 identical sets. Each person gets a set. Instead of household items, you can use natural items like twigs, pinecones, stones, leaves, shells, seed pods, flowers, feathers or nuts.

- Remove the lid of the cardboard box so that there are just 4 sides and a bottom on the box. With partners sitting facing each other, stand the box up between the two partners with the open side facing one partner.

- The partner with the open box side facing them will be the "communicator." He/she arranges the objects in their set inside of the box so that the other partner, the "listener," cannot see the arrangement.

- When finished arranging, the communicator draws pictures or uses words to describe the arrangement of objects to the listener.

- Without peeking, the listener follows the communicator's directions to repeat the arrangement, pattern, or construction using their own, second set of objects. The communicator can use only words or pictures and may not use hand gestures.

- When finished, turn the box to reveal the hidden arrangement. Do they match?

- Try it again with partners switching roles.

Next

- For a challenge, increase the number of objects or limit the time or number of words used to describe object arrangements.

- Choose one of the objects to describe from a different viewpoint. For example, describe it from a magnified, reversed, distant, top or underside view. Your partner tries to determine which object you are describing and/or which viewpoint you are using.

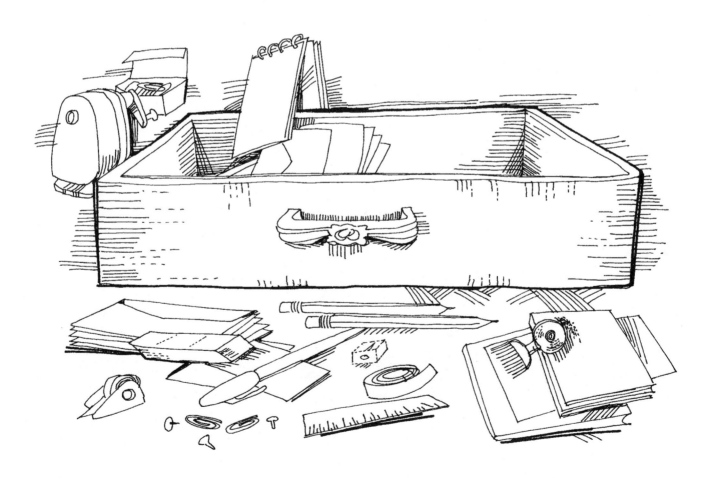

CHAPTER 5

OBSERVING YOUR WORLD

Observation Series

Supplies

- *9 or more objects from a household drawer, purse, backpack, etc.*

- *3 large, paper grocery bags*

- *pencils*

- *3 sheets of newspaper*

- *paper*

- *timer (kitchen timer, clock or watch with second hand)*

- *scissors*

- *ruler*

- *8 or more non-identical samples of the same type of object (rocks, pencils, beans, bottle caps, silverware, leaves, sea shells, etc.)*

Why

To practice careful observation and accurate recording.

When

Ancient societies lived closer to nature than most people do today. Long ago, observing plants, animals, insects, birds, the weather, and other natural phenomena was part of daily life. Over thousands of years, information about the world gained through observation has been passed from one person to the next. Observation has aided many people in predicting events, providing food, and keeping them safe.

What

We use our senses (sight, smell, taste, touch, hearing) to make observations. The ability to make accurate observations is an important science skill. An observation yields information that can be measured or detected directly with the senses or with an instrument that enhances our senses, like a microscope. An inference is an interpretation or explanation of an observation. We use our observations to make inferences. For example, people who track animals make inferences about the direction an animal is going or what is causing it to leave a certain type of track. The number, age, weight, sex, and behavior of animals can be inferred by careful observation of the tracks left behind. A quantitative observation includes numbers such as mass, length, and quantity. A qualitative observation includes descriptive words, like color or shape. Your observations should include as much information as possible so that you do not overlook anything that later may turn out to be significant.

How

Follow the directions for each observation activity using the supplies listed.

Seeing and Remembering

In this activity, make timed observations, and then try to remember what you saw.

- Collect a group of 9 or more household objects.

- Open the seams of a large, paper grocery bag to make a large sheet.

- Draw a 4 by 4 square grid on the bag. Each grid section should be large enough to hold 1 of the household objects.

- Have one person secretly place the objects on the grid, and then cover everything with a sheet of newspaper. Some spaces may be left empty.

- Ask each family member to draw a small similar grid on a sheet of paper.

- Set a timer for 1 minute. Uncover the objects.

- Each person should observe the objects but may not write anything down. When the time is up, cover the objects.

- Ask each person to write the names of the objects on their grid, trying to get them in the correct location.

- When everyone is finished, uncover the objects and have each person compare his/her grid with the objects on the paper bag grid.

- The person with the most objects listed or with the most objects listed in the correct position arranges and covers the objects for another round.

- Increase or decrease the number of objects or the amount of observation time to vary the challenge.

Observation Frame

- Make 2 different size paper frames. Cut a small square about 1 by 1 inch (2.5 by 2.5 centimeters) from the center of 1 sheet of newspaper. In the center of another sheet, cut a larger square about 4 by 4 inches (10 by 10 centimeters).

- Find an interesting place indoors or outdoors to lay down the newspaper frame with the smaller opening. For example, try it over the sidewalk, grass, dirt, dinner table, work area, kitchen floor, carpet, etc.

- Make a list of everything you observe when looking through the smaller opening.

- Change to the sheet with the larger opening. Place the sheet in such a way as to include the earlier 1 inch square observation area. Add new observations to the first list.

Search

The challenge is to use a written description to identify an object.

- Put objects that are the same type (different size rocks or sea shells) but not identical in a bag.

- Use twice as many objects as you have people. For example, if you have 6 people in your group, put 12 rocks in the bag.

- Have each person pick 1 object from the bag, and then write a description of the object without using its actual name.

- When everyone is finished, return the objects to the bag, and put the descriptions in another bag.

- Next, spread the objects out on the table.

- Take turns reading the descriptions. Try to find the object that matches each description.

- Discuss which type of information is most helpful in identifying an object. Describe the skills you used to observe, record and identify your object. What tools would be helpful in making observations?

Looking Through a Water Drop

Age:
5-13
Participants:
Group, Family, Pair

Why

To construct a simple tool that enhances observation.

Who

You'll try to read these sentences later with your water drop magnifier.

The first woman ever invited to join the American Academy of Sciences was Maria Mitchell, an astronomer. The first American Indian woman doctor in the United States was Susan LaFlesche. Katherine Johnson, an outstanding African American space scientist, was a recipient of a group achievement award presented by NASA's Lunar Spacecraft and Operations Team.

How

In this activity, looking through a drop of water will magnify what you see about 4 times.

- Flatten a small cardboard box. Cut a 2 by 2 inch (5 by 5 centimeter) square from the cardboard.

- Using a standard hole punch, punch a hole in the center of the cardboard square.

- Cover the hole with transparent tape. This is your water drop lens. The hole will be your viewing window.

- Set the water drop lens down on a sheet of newspaper with the sticky side of the tape facing down. Position the hole over a letter.

- Dip a pencil point in water. Carefully drop water on the lens above the hole until it covers the viewing window.

- Look through the water drop. Slowly move the lens away from and toward the paper to discover which position gives the best view. Compare what you see through the lens with the letters not under the lens.

- The water drop lens is portable, so you can continue making observations elsewhere on the paper. Hold the lens gently between your thumb and index finger as you move to another area of the newspaper.

Supplies

- *empty cardboard box from cereal, crackers, tissues, pasta, etc.*
- *scissors*
- *ruler*
- *pencil*
- *hole punch*
- *transparent tape, not frosted*
- *sheet of newspaper*
- *water*

- Try reading the information printed in very small type under the "Who" heading on the previous page. Newspaper weather forecasts and information on the financial pages also work well since they are usually printed in small type.
- What are some things you noticed looking through the water drop that you didn't see before?

Next

- Put a piece of tape directly onto a section of small print in the newspaper.
- Dip a pencil into a container of water. Hold the pencil close to the place you've covered with tape. Let the water drip off the pencil until the drop is about 1/2 inch (1 centimeter) in diameter. How does what you see through this "fixed" water lens compare with what you saw through the "portable" lens?

Will it Grow?

Why

To investigate seed germination and plant growth.

When

Learning about Aztec civilization usually includes mention of gold, pyramids and conquests. However, not everyone knows that Aztec gardeners cultivated a wide variety of medicinal plants. Ancient books, such as the *Florentine Codex* and the *Badianus Codex*, describe plants of ancient times and how people used them medicinally. Modern biochemistry confirms that such plants do play a role in helping to cure illness.

What

Most plants grow from seeds. Most seeds are the parts of flowering plants that contain the plant embryo. The embryo uses the food inside the seed as it grows. After a seed sprouts, it uses the sun's energy to produce food and oxygen from water and carbon dioxide. This process is called photosynthesis.

The major parts of a plant are roots, stems, and leaves. Roots anchor the plant in soil, store food, and absorb water and minerals. The stem supports the plant, transports water and nutrients to the leaves, and stores food. Photosynthesis takes place in the leaves.

How

Germination

Build a container to germinate bean seeds.

- Have an adult cut a 2 liter plastic soft drink bottle in half.
- Set the top half inside the bottom with the spout down.
- Add water to the bottom half until it reaches the spout.
- Lift out the spout section. Pull a corner of a paper towel from the inside of the spout section through the spout about 2.5 inches (6 centimeters).
- Return the top half to the bottom half. The pulled corner of the paper towel should be in the water.
- Set 3 to 4 bean seeds inside the container on top of the paper towel.

Supplies

- *2 liter clear, plastic soft drink bottle*
- *utility knife*
- *water*
- *white paper towels*
- *seeds: bean, pumpkin, grass, radish, lettuce, flower (at least 6 of each)*
- *paper*
- *pencils*
- *2 clear plastic cups, the same size*
- *transparent tape*
- *permanent felt-tip marker*
- *egg carton*
- *scissors*
- *fork*
- *large spoon*
- *soil, about 2 cups*

- Cover the seeds with another paper towel.
- Draw a diagram in your journal of the finished germinator.
- Each day check the germinator and look at the seeds. Use words and pictures to keep a record of your observations.

Sprouting

Construct a container to observe the stem and root sprout from a pumpkin seed.

- Fold a paper towel in half lengthwise, and then wet it. Wrap it around the outside of a transparent cup, keeping it even with the bottom.
- Fill another transparent cup about 1/4 full of water.
- Press the pumpkin seeds onto the wet paper towel. Arrange the seeds in different positions around the sides of the cup. Leave some space between each seed.
- Carefully slide the seed cup into the water cup, until the bottom of the seed cup touches the water.
- Using a permanent felt pen, label each seed with a number by writing on the outside of the water cup.
- Draw a picture in your journal of each numbered seed. Predict the place you think the stem and root will begin sprouting. Label these locations on your drawing.
- Check the seeds every day for changes. Use words and pictures to describe the changes. Record the date and time of your observations.
- Keep the paper towel wet by tipping the cup from side to side.
- When the roots and stem appear, compare your predictions with what really happens.
- Next, draw arrows on your picture to point which direction you think the root and stem will continue to grow.
- Continue checking the seeds each day for changes. Keep the paper towel wet by tipping the cup.
- If the soil outside is warm enough, you can plant the sprouting seeds in an outdoor garden.

Planting

- Collect 6 different types of seeds, 5 of each type.
- Tape a sample of each seed on a sheet of paper and label it.
- Cut the lid off an egg carton. Use a fork to poke holes in the bottom of the egg cups for drainage.
- Fill each egg cup with soil.

- Have one person plant 2 seeds of each type in the 6 cups on one side of the carton. Keep a record in your journal of which seeds are planted in each cup.

- Ask a partner to plant 2 seeds of each type in the cups on the opposite side. Write your names on the carton to label each set of seeds.

- Put the carton in the lid to catch the water flowing through.

- Add enough water to soak the soil. Place in a sunny location.

- Check daily for plant growth. Keep the soil moist, but not soggy.

- Compare the plants on each side of the carton. Which plants are the same?

- Use your journal notes to match the seeds to the plants.

- Record the results in your journal.

Did you know..?
Thomas Wyatt Turner was a pioneer in studying the effect of mineral nutrients on seed plants. He experimented with cotton breeding and was the chair of the Biology Department at the Hampton Institute.

Web Building

Supplies

- *2 sturdy chairs for each web*
- *yarn, 2 different colors*
- *scissors*
- *newspaper*

Why

To explore the relationship between structure and function in nature.

What

A spider's body has 2 parts, a head and an abdomen. They have 4 pairs of segmented legs, a pair of pedipalps, 4 pairs of eyes, and a pair of chelicerae attached to their heads. The pedipalps are used for grasping, and the chelicerae are used for piercing prey.

Most spiders use silk to travel, mark a path, store food, protect their eggs, and construct webs. Orb webs are efficient structures covering a large area with a small amount of silk. Silk is secreted through spinnerets located at the end of the abdomen. Spiders can control the diameter and elasticity of their silk.

Structures in nature have a design, perform a function and use a variety of materials. Many natural structures have provided models or inspiration for human made structures. Just as in nature, structures support every form of human activity.

How

Construct an orb-shaped web, like the ones a garden spider builds.

- Look for a location with room to work and places to attach yarn. For example, 2 sturdy chairs placed at least 1 yard (1 meter) apart would work well.
- The first step in building a web is to construct a framework. The rest of the web will be woven inside this framework. Stretch a length of yarn between the 2 chairs to form a bridge. Tie off each end to a different chair.
- Tie a new length of yarn to each end of the bridge. Attach the untied end of each strand to a new point. Continue by adding additional lengths of yarn to the ends of each new side of the framework until you have a closed shape with 3, 4, or 5 sides.
- Next, construct the orb-shaped part of the web inside the framework. Add another length of yarn from the center of the bridge, and tie it to an edge of the frame.
- Continue adding radial strands, working from the center out, alternating from side to side to keep the web balanced. Be sure

FAMILY SCIENCE

all strands are taut. For your web to function, you need at least 6 radial strands.

- Starting close to the center, weave a short strand of yarn in and out of the radial strands going twice around the circle to create a hub. This forms a work platform for the spider, and it helps hold the radial strands in place until the web is completed.

- The silk the spider uses for the orb is usually sticky, so use a different color yarn for this next part of your web. Roll the second color of yarn into a small ball.

- Work from the outside of the framework toward the center. To start, tie the yarn to the framework. Begin spiraling in toward the center, wrapping the yarn around each radial strand as you cross it.

- When you reach the hub, tie the yarn to the hub to hold it in place. Your orb web is finished.
- To test how well your web detects prey, tie a length of yarn to the hub. This is the signal line.
- Crumple a sheet of newspaper into a fist size ball. The ball is the spider's prey.
- One person volunteers to be the spider. With eyes closed, the spider should hold the signal line taut.
- Another person tosses the prey at the web. Ask the spider to call out when he/she feels the prey hitting the web.
- Take turns being the spider. Try larger and smaller prey to compare how they feel when they hit the web.

Did you know..?

Navajo legend describes Spiderwoman as a kindly goddess who lived in the ground. Taking pity on a lost Navajo maiden, the goddess blew open a hole in the ground wide enough for the girl to enter. Before showing the girl the way back, Spiderwoman taught her the art of spinning. Today Navajo weavers leave a tiny spider's hole in their blankets for good luck.

Research has proven that spiders coat their webs with fungicides and bactericides to protect their webs from fungi and bacteria. Thousands of years ago, people used spider silk as a dressing for wounds to prevent infection. Recently, scientists have produced spider silk in the laboratory, which can be passed through a hollow needle creating threads like spiders do through their spinnerets. These threads may be woven or bonded to create products for research or industry.

Dr. Catherine Craig, while studying spider webs, discovered that webs are not passive structures. Spiders use attractive zigzag designs and colors to attract insects to their webs. These patterns are visible to feeding insects but not people.

Map Habitats

Supplies

- *road map, preferably one with many colors*
- *tape*
- *3 sheets of paper, in colors similar to those on the road map*
- *scissors*
- *ruler*
- *cup*
- *1 piece blank paper*
- *tweezers, optional*
- *watch with a second hand*
- *pencil*
- *copies of 1 Centimeter Graph Paper*
- *crayons*

Why

To explore the protective coloration of prey.
To construct a bar graph.

What

Predators and prey are linked together in food chains. Predators feed on prey. Many predators are also prey to other predators.

One way prey and predators survive is by blending into their habitat. The color and patterns of their coverings provide protection for the prey and can help hide the predator.

The number of predators and prey in a habitat is important to the growth and survival of each one. A lack of predators will result in an increase in the prey population. In an environment with too few prey, the predator may not survive. In this activity, participants will be predators, collect prey and record the results.

A map is a flat diagram of an area on the earth's surface. Maps use symbols, lines, patterns and color to represent three dimensional features. A line may indicate a road, a state boundary, or an elevation change. However, the size, shape and color of each line will be different for each one. On a map, a legend explains the symbols, diagrams and other reference information. During this activity, the map will represent an environment for exploring protective coloration.

How

In this activity, family members are the predators looking for food. Prey are paper squares. A road map is the habitat.

- Open the road map on a table. You may want to tape it down to keep it from moving.

- Find 3 sheets of paper that match 3 colors on the map. Pink, red, white, blue, green and yellow are common map colors.

- To make prey, cut 20, 1/2 inch (1 centimeter) squares from each color of paper. Fold each square in half. This will make the prey easier to pick up.

- Put all of the prey into a cup; then shake the cup to mix them up.

- Sprinkle the prey over the entire map.

- On each turn, one person is a timekeeper and another person is the predator.

- Place a blank sheet of paper along the side of the map to collect the prey.

- The predator will use his/her fingers or tweezers to pick up the prey one at a time and put them on the blank paper.

- The predator collects prey for 30 seconds. The timekeeper announces when to start and stop.

- Together, separate the prey by color and count them. In your journal, record the numbers of each prey color collected.

- Return the prey to the cup, and then scatter them on the map again.

- Each predator collects prey 3 times for 30 seconds each time.

- Calculate the average number of each color of prey the predator collected. Total the number of each color and divide by 3 to calculate the average.

- Switch roles and repeat the activity.

- Make a bar graph to compare the number of prey of each type collected.

- To make a bar graph, copy the *1 Centimeter Graph Paper* on page 127 and label each of the prey colors along the horizontal line at the bottom of the graph paper.

- Starting at the bottom left, number the boxes along the vertical side from 1 to 20.

- With crayons, color the number of boxes above each prey color that corresponds to the average number you collected.

- The bar graph compares the average number of each type of prey collected during the same length of time. The bar graph makes it easy to see patterns. This may be helpful in predicting future events. For instance, discuss which prey has the best chance of survival in your habitat. Which has the least chance of survival? Why are there differences?

Next

- You may want to challenge other participants by making new prey with more protective coloration. Repeat the experiment. Make a bar graph to display the results. Compare the new results with your first experiment.

- Use the same prey on a different map. Discuss any difference in the results.

FAMILY SCIENCE

- Start by scattering 60 prey, 20 of each color on the map. Your partner says stop when you have collected half of the prey, 30. Count the number of each color collected, and then put them aside. Sort and count the prey still on the map. Make additional prey so you can double the number of each type of prey remaining on the map. Then shake, scatter, and repeat. What is happening to the prey population?

- For an even greater challenge, obtain two identical maps. Cut your prey squares out of one map. After folding, scatter the prey on the whole map. Is there any change in difficulty finding the prey?

1 Centimeter Graph Paper

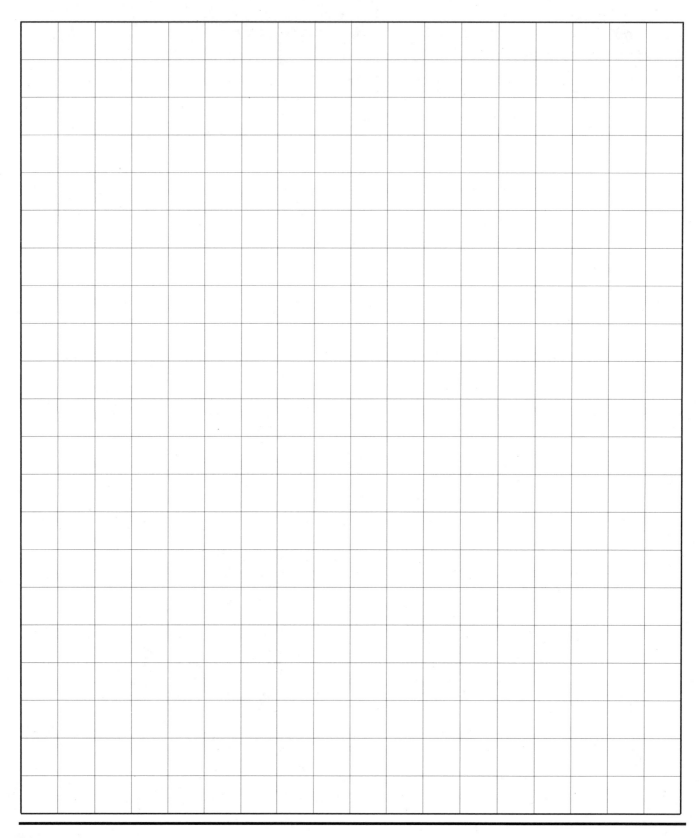

FAMILY SCIENCE

Earful

Supplies

- *blindfold (optional)*
- *sound producer (small bell, empty tin can, etc.)*
- *playing cards, or other items to use as "markers"*
- *construction paper, 9 x 12 inches or larger*
- *scissors*
- *pencil*
- *tape*
- *tape measure*

Why

To explore the limits of your hearing.
To design a structure to improve your hearing.

What

People have fixed outer ears that act as sound collectors, helping to funnel sounds into the ear canal. At the end of the ear canal is the eardrum. Sound waves trigger vibrations of the eardrum which your brain then interprets as sound. If you cup your hand behind your ears, distant sounds will seem louder because you have captured and funneled more sound waves into your ear canal. In this activity, you will design a new outer ear to catch more sound.

How

This activity needs to be done in a large space indoors or outdoors.

- Before you begin, find something that will produce a soft sound with the same volume each time you use it. It should be something you can carry, like a small bell, tin can or retractable ball-point pen.

- Divide into pairs. Assign one person to be the listener and another person to be the sound maker.

- The listener stands in one spot without moving, eyes closed (or blindfolded). The sound maker stands approximately 3 feet (1 meter) away and makes a sound. The listener points in the direction of the sound.

- The sound maker then moves around the room, closer and farther from the listener, making the same sound at various points. The listener points in the direction of the sound each time. The sound maker can measure the range of the listener's hearing by dropping a playing card face up, or other marker, at each spot where the listener heard the sound and pointed in the right direction. When the listener can't hear the sound or points in the wrong direction, the sound maker drops a playing card face down.

- Using a tape measure, calculate the distance from the listener to the face down cards. Record this distance as the "maximum" range for your partner to detect the sound. Repeat the procedure for each partner. Record your results in your journal.

- Next, use construction paper to build 2 structures that will fit around the outside of your ears to increase the range and amount of sound you hear.

- When your new pair of ears is ready, try them on to make sure they fit. Make adjustments.

- Repeat the activity again, but this time wear the new outer ears.

- Once the sound maker has established the listener's new range, compare it to the original range. Did the new outer ears help improve the listener's hearing?

- Be sure to switch roles and try it again.

Next

- Now that you've tried one new design for your outer ear, do you think you could improve your range with another design? Try it!

Did you know..?

Bats are the only mammals that can fly. Many bats eat insects at night near ponds, streams, forests, cliffs, buildings, bridges and other human-made structures. Bats guide themselves toward food and away from obstacles using sound. The high frequency sounds they produce through their mouths and nostrils bounce off the obstacles around them. Using echoes, bats can determine the presence, distance, direction, velocity, size, shape and texture of the objects around them. Learning more about the echolocation system of bats has been helpful to scientists who develop ultrasonic orientation systems for the blind.

CHAPTER 6

THE PHYSICAL WORLD

Tube Planetarium

Supplies

- *empty toilet paper tubes (about 6/participant)*
- *scissors*
- *copy of Constellation Circles*
- *rubber bands or tape*
- *push pins*
- *penlight or small flashlight 1 1/2 inches (3.8 centimeters) or less in diameter*

Why

To explore astronomy by constructing a simple apparatus and learning about constellations.

When

The Dogon people of West Africa were performing astronomical research as far back as 700 years ago. Dogon astronomer-priests gained a rich knowledge of the heavens without modern equipment, such as the powerful telescopes we use today. These early astronomers determined the orbital cycles of Jupiter and Saturn, the rings and moons of Saturn, the structure of the Milky Way, and the spiral path of the Moon. They also studied the brightest star in the sky, Sirius, which is part of the constellation we call Canis Major, or "Big Dog."

What

Without expensive equipment, you can learn the locations and shapes of the constellations and map the night sky. A constellation is a group of stars whose pattern represents the outline of a figure. Throughout history, people used their imagination when observing constellations in order to name them after recognizable objects, animals or mythological figures. Knowing how a constellation got its name can add to the fun of finding them up above!

How

- Copy and cut out the 6 *Constellation Circles* (see page 135).

- Center 1 circle face-out on the end of each toilet paper tube. Fold down the edges around the tube and use tape or a rubber band to hold it in place. You may want to write the name of the constellation on the side of the tube.

- Use a push pin to poke holes through each star mark. The large dots are very bright stars. Make the holes for the brighter stars a little larger.

- Find a dark place to view your constellation. Check to make sure the flashlight works before you go into a dark room, closet, or under a table.

- Hold the tube with the constellation circle pointing up. Push the flashlight into the open end of the tube. Move the flashlight up and down inside the tube and experiment with various angles to get the best image of your constellation on the ceiling.

- Adjust the flashlight until you see the constellation clearly. The constellation will be difficult to see if there is too much light in the room, not enough light from the flashlight, or if the flashlight is moving.

Next

- Borrow a library book, check newsstands for an astronomy magazine, or surf the World Wide Web to learn the location of your constellations at different times of the year. Can you find them in the night sky?

- Team up with other family members to project each constellation on the ceiling in the locations as they appear in the night sky.

- Visit a science museum, planetarium or astronomy club to help expand your study of astronomy and constellations.

- Make additional constellation diagrams for your collection.

- Find out how American Indians and other indigenous people explored the night sky.

Did you know..?

Maria Mitchell (1818–88) was an astronomer whose interest in stars and planets began when she was a child. Together with her father, an amateur astronomer, she learned how to use scientific equipment to collect information about stars, planets and the sky. Later, as a librarian, she read advanced astronomical texts and continued her sky observations. In 1847, she used a telescope to discover the first comet. The American Academy of Sciences recognized her achievement by accepting her as their first woman member. She continued her work in astronomy as a professor at Vassar College, guiding other women in the study of astronomy.

Constellation Circles

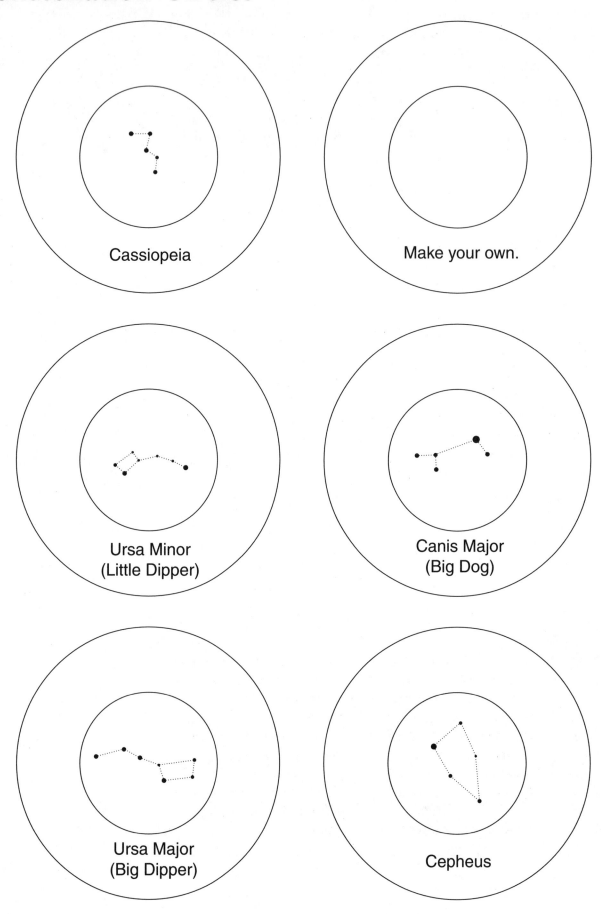

Cassiopeia

Make your own.

Ursa Minor
(Little Dipper)

Canis Major
(Big Dog)

Ursa Major
(Big Dipper)

Cepheus

FAMILY SCIENCE

Bubble Windows

Age:
5-13
Participants:
Group, Family, Pair

Why

To explore the properties of soap film.

What

A soap bubble has thin, flexible walls. Soap film is elastic. When you blow on a soap bubble, you can see the soap film expand and contract. A bubble stretches to cover the largest area with the least amount of soap solution. In this activity, you will explore the elasticity of soap film by adding movable parts to a bubble wand.

How

- In the measuring cup, slowly stir 2 tablespoons of liquid soap into 1 cup of water to make the bubble solution.

- Cut off the bottom of the plastic cup. Next, cut 2 straight lines (about 1/2 inch apart) from the bottom to within a 1/2 inch (1 centimeter) of the rim.

- Cut around the rim between the 2 straight cuts. When you're finished cutting, bend the strip back to make a handle. This is your bubble wand.

Supplies

- *liquid measuring cup*
- *measuring spoons*
- *liquid dish soap*
- *water*
- *8 or 10 ounce disposable plastic cups (thin enough to cut with scissors)*
- *scissors*
- *thread*
- *needle*
- *shallow containers (pie tins, cookie sheets)*

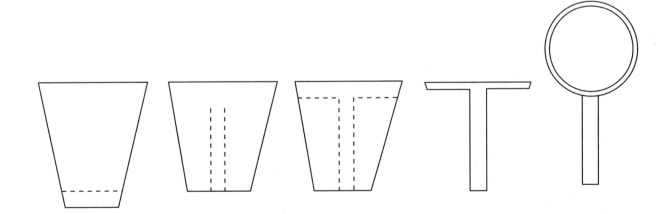

- Cut 2 pieces of thread about 8 inches (20 centimeters) long.

- Thread the needle and don't tie a knot in the thread. To secure the thread to one spot on the rim, push the needle through the rim of the bubble wand halfway between the handle and the top of the circle. Pull the thread only part way through leaving just enough to tie the thread securely around the rim. Remove the needle.

- Tie a loop the size of your finger on the end of the other thread.

- Thread the needle. Push the needle and thread through the end of the handle and pull through approximately 2 inches (5 centimeters) of thread. Remove the needle and tie a knot in the thread.

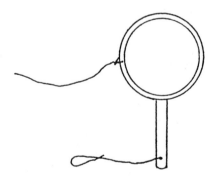

- Pour the bubble solution into a shallow container.

- Dip the wand into the soap solution, and then lift it up. The soap film will be stretched flat across the opening.

- Stretch the rim thread across the center of the opening, and then dip again. When you lift it, the thread will stick to the soap film. Hold onto the thread.

- Ask your partner to pop the soap film above the thread with a dry finger.

FAMILY SCIENCE

- The soap film will fill half of the opening. Slide the thread along the rim. This will stretch the soap film so you can fill the wand completely. Practice until it works each time.

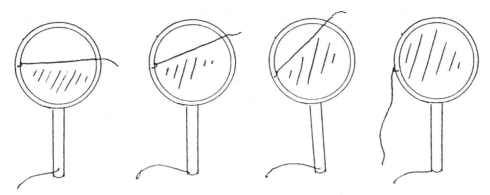

- Dip and lift the wand again. This time let go of the thread before your partner pops it.

- The soap film will pull the thread over to the rim. Holding the loose end of the thread, slide it along the rim to fill the opening. Take turns with your partner.

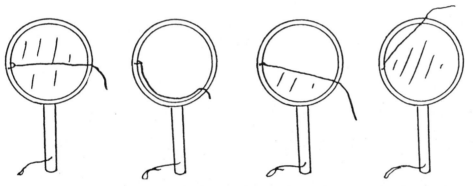

- Dip the looped thread and wand into the solution. The looped thread will stick to the soap film when you lift it.

- Discuss what will happen when you pop the center of the loop, and then try it.

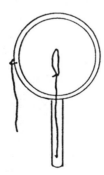

Next

- Add threads to create new windows. Record your new shapes, sizes and methods. Using your wand, what other properties can you discover about bubbles and soap film?

Common Properties

Supplies

- *an assortment of common house-hold items such as: bottle cap, button, small ball of modeling clay, cork, crayon, sheet of aluminum foil, marble, paper clip, penny, rubber band, sponge, plastic soda straw, toothpick, plastic container with lid (Note: all items will get wet)*

- *large sheet of paper, paper bag, or wax paper*

- *felt pen*

- *cardboard, at least 6 x 12 inches (15 x 30 cm)*

- *index cards*

- *scissors*

- *bowl*

Why

To explore the properties of common materials.
To identify and control variables in an experiment.

Who

Venn diagrams are named for John Venn, an English mathematician who lived between 1834-1923. Venn diagrams use pictures, which often include overlapping circles, to show what sets of objects have in common. For example, some seashells are all white. Others are smooth on the outside. Some are both all white and smooth. A Venn diagram demonstrates the relationship between these sets as follows:

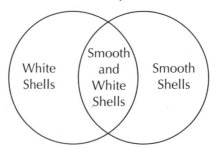

What

Properties are characteristics of an object that can be used to describe it. For example, words that describe the properties of this sheet of paper are white, smooth, and thin. Exploring properties is one way to learn about the physical world. In the following activities, your family will identify the properties of materials, and then sort the materials based on those properties.

How

- Describe the properties of the objects in your collection.

- Draw a large Venn diagram on the large paper with a felt pen, like this:

FAMILY SCIENCE

- Position the Venn diagram on the table so that everyone can reach it.

- When you're ready, pick one of the following activities to continue learning about the properties of your objects.

Roll and Slide

- Build an inclined plane with cardboard. An inclined plane is a flat surface that is neither horizontal nor vertical but slanted.

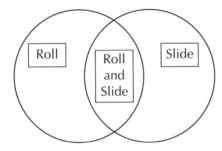

- Make paper labels for each section of the Venn diagram and place them as shown above.

- Each person chooses a household item to test. Write the name of your item on an index card.

- Before you begin testing, each person should predict how his/her object will move on the inclined plane. Place the object cards on the Venn diagram in the section that corresponds to your predictions.

- After the objects are sorted, test each one by releasing it from the top of the inclined plane.

- After testing, move each item to the section of the Venn Diagram that describes how it moved. How did your test results compare with your predictions?

- What might affect the results of your tests? (For example, does the size of the object affect the results? How about the way it is placed on the incline plane?)

- Compare your results with other families or groups, and discuss how to control the variable factors. (Variables are things that change or can be changed.)

Sink and Float

- Buoyancy is the upward force of a fluid on objects in the fluid. An object sinks because the weight of the fluid that the object pushes aside is less than the weight of the object itself.

- Label the Venn diagram as shown:

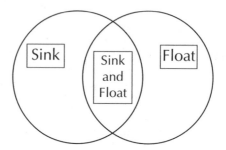

- Fill a bowl with water.

- After choosing an object to test, write the object's name on an index card.

- Predict whether your object will sink or float and put the card in the appropriate place on the Venn diagram.

- Test each item and then place the object in the appropriate place on the Venn diagram. How did your test results compare with your predictions?

- List the variable factors that affected your results, and compare them with the roll and slide test. What patterns do you see in the variables listed for both tests?

Next

- Predict whether objects will sink or float in saltwater. Salt changes the density of water. Saltwater is denser than fresh water. This greater density produces a larger upward force on a floating object. Try the "Sink and Float" test using saltwater. How do your results compare with your predictions? Compare your results with your freshwater results.

- Put a sheet of paper at the end of the inclined plane. Secure the paper to your surface using tape. Place a sliding object at the top. Compare how far each object slides by marking on the paper where the object stops. Repeat with a rolling object, recording how far it rolls on the paper. Measure the distance between the end of the ramp and the marks to compare the results. What patterns do you see, if any, between the objects and how far they moved?

Did you know..?

Fishing is an activity that combines sinking and floating materials to successfully catch fish. Most fishing lines, nets and hooks float in water. Different weights are combined with the floating materials to pull them under the surface.

Modern sinkers are made from lead. In the past, Polynesian cultures shaped a variety of stone sinkers from basalt or reef rock. In the Hawaiian Islands, the sinkers were used for net and deep sea fishing. Weighing from 1 ounce to 6 pounds, they enabled people to fish 400 fathoms (2,400 feet or 731 meters) deep in the ocean.

Charge It

Supplies

- *masking tape*
- *ruler*
- *2 empty aluminum cans*
- *4 balloons*
- *1 yard (1 meter) of string*
- *scissors*
- *thread*

Why

To explore electrical charges that can push and pull.

What

Electrical charges are either positive or negative. Protons carry positive charge, while electrons carry negative electrical charge. Opposite charges, a positive and a negative, attract each other. Similar charges, like two positives, repel each other.

Scientists believe that under certain conditions, objects lose or gain electrons. One way to change the charge on an object is to rub it rapidly against other objects. For example, when you rub a balloon with a wool sock, some of the socks' electrons transfer to the balloon, increasing the number of electrons on the balloon. What happens? The balloon now has a negative charge and the sock has a positive charge, and they attract each other.

How

In this activity, you will experiment with static electricity. Your local weather may affect the results of these activities. It is easier to produce static electricity in a cool, dry climate. When the weather is wet or humid, it is difficult for objects to hold an electrical charge because the increased water vapor in the air tends to pull the charge away from the object.

Recycled Can Race

Have a race using static electricity to move objects.

- Using masking tape, mark a "start" and a "finish" line on the floor about 1 yard (1 meter) apart.

- Place 2 empty soft drink cans on their sides on the starting line.

- Inflate and tie-off 2 balloons. To charge the balloons, rub them rapidly back and forth on your clothing for a minute.

- When you're ready for the race, hold the balloons near the cans, without touching them to the cans, and have someone say "go."

- Each person tries to move his/her can across the finish line using only the static electricity of the balloon.

- After the race, ask participants to identify whether the part of the can nearest the balloon had similar or opposite charges. How could they tell?

Balloon Pendants

- Inflate 2 balloons, and then tie the balloons on opposite ends of a 1 yard (1 meter) string.

- Stretch the string between 2 people. Each person rubs a balloon back and forth rapidly on his/her clothing or hair.

- As each person holds onto his/her balloon, one of them grabs the center of the string.

- What do you think will happen when each person drops his/her balloon? Try it.

- Why did this happen?

Stand Up

- Cut a length of thread about 8 inches (20 centimeters) long. At the end of the thread, tie a loop large enough for one of your fingers, and then slip it on.

- Rub an inflated balloon rapidly against your clothing. Rubbing the balloon gives it an electrical charge.

- Hold the balloon near the loose end of the thread and see what happens. Then move the thread farther from the balloon.

- Can you explain what happened and why?

What Would Happen If...

Supplies

- *felt pen*
- *nickel*
- *recycled plastic lid*
- *scissors*
- *hole punch*
- *copy of Will It Move? sheet*
- *2 paper clips*
- *spool of thread*
- *rubber bands, a variety of sizes*
- *pencil*
- *safety glasses recommended*

Why

To assemble a simple device.
To explore potential and kinetic energy.

What

Objects can store energy in many ways. A twisted rubber band stores elastic potential energy. A boulder sitting on top of a mountain stores gravitational potential energy because of its distance from the ground below. When an object moves, the stored potential energy becomes kinetic energy. In this activity, you will construct a simple device to experiment with kinetic energy and elastic potential energy.

How

- Trace 2 circles the size of a nickel on the plastic lid. Cut out the circles, and then punch a hole in the center of each.

- Cut apart the cards on the *"Will It Move?"* sheet (see page 146). Arrange the steps in order, and follow the diagrams to create your experimental device.

- After playing with your device, try making changes to the design. Consult the "What would happen if..." chart below for ideas. Fill in the chart while you test each design.

What would happen if...

the pencil was shorter?	
the rubber band was longer?	
the rubber band was shorter?	
the floor was smooth?	
the floor was textured?	
there were no plastic washers?	

Will It Move?

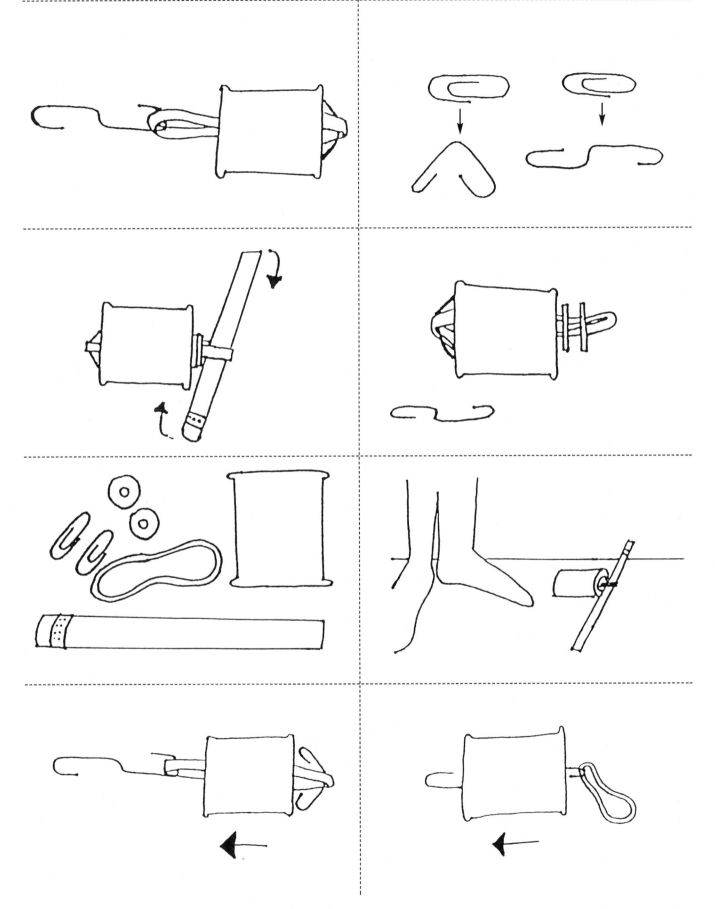

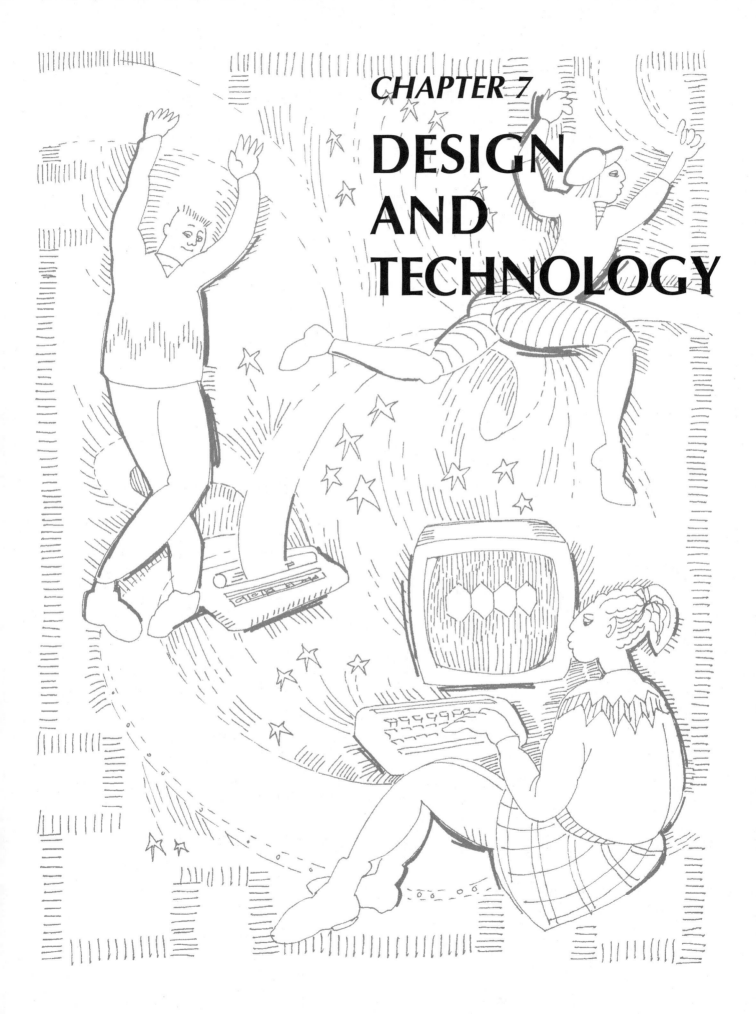

CHAPTER 7
DESIGN AND TECHNOLOGY

Bubble Construction

Supplies

- *scissors*
- *large plastic trash bag*
- *paper towels*
- *water*
- *measuring spoons*
- *liquid dish soap*
- *liquid measuring cup*
- *empty gallon milk jug (needed only for large group)*
- *ruler*
- *corrugated cardboard box*
- *newspaper*
- *plastic bowl or tray*
- *copy of Bubble Construction Chart*
- *tool construction supplies (string, pipe cleaners, aluminum foil, stiff paper, cardboard, recycled containers, plastic straws, paper or plastic cups)*
- *pencil*
- *paper*

Why

To design tools to create a specific "bubble" product.

What

Manufacturing is the production of items by hand or machine. Most often, manufacturing is associated with large scale production in which the labor is divided into different tasks. In this activity, your family will design tools to manufacture "bubble" products using common, household objects.

How

Prepare the Construction Site

- Make a large table cover by cutting the side seams of a trash bag. Open it flat. Wipe the table with a damp paper towel, and then spread the cover over the damp area.

- Mix a bubble solution by combining 2 tablespoons of liquid dish soap with 1 cup of water. To make a larger amount, pour 2/3 cup of liquid dish soap into an empty gallon milk jug, and then fill with water. Mix the solution by stirring slowly. Try to keep bubbles and foam from forming on the surface.

- Cut the cardboard box into sections about 6 by 8 inches (15 by 20 centimeters). Make one for each person. You will use the cardboard as squeegees to clear extra liquid away from the work area.

- Have sheets of newspaper or a roll of paper towels nearby to soak up spills or to blot an area dry. Plain vinegar also works well to break down the soap and help clean off the work surface.

- Put supplies and tools in the center of the work area. Pour a small amount of bubble solution into a bowl or tray.

FAMILY SCIENCE

Bubble Production

- Distribute one *Bubble Construction Chart* (see page 151) to each family or group.

- Each group selects one of the bubble products to produce. As a team, they will first design a tool that will produce the bubble product, and then record their method for others to follow.

- Choose the type of materials the group needs to construct the tool.

- Assemble and test the tool until the group produces consistent results. Remember, the goal is to produce a bubble product as described on the construction chart.

- Once you have perfected your method, write step-by-step directions to explain how to produce your bubble product. Give the directions to someone else. Do they get the same results?

- Continue the design and production of the other bubble products. Fill in the chart while you work.

- Keep your chart on a separate, dry surface while you test your bubble production tools.

Bubble Construction Chart

Design Brief: Design a tool to create each of the specific bubble products listed below.

Product	Materials Used To Make Tool	Tool Design Diagram (Draw your tool)	Production Notes/Testing (How does your tool work?)
floating sphere A floating round figure with the appearance of a globe or ball.			
stationary sphere A fixed round figure with the appearance of a globe or ball.			
hemisphere A half of a sphere.			
concentric Three or more circles having a center in common.			
cylinder A hollow figure with ends that are parallel and equal circles on each end.			
cluster A number of items grouped together.			
chain A continuous connected line.			

Stretching the Limits

Why

To produce a change by combining substances.
To design a product to meet specifications.

What

Borax is a mineral that's found in deserts where the evaporation of salt lakes and seeping water have left deposits. The word "borax" comes from the Persian word, "burah," which means white. Today, we use borax as a rust inhibitor, water softener, and household bleach. It's also used in paints, adhesives and detergents. This activity uses borax to explore chemistry by making an interesting substance called "Creep."

How

- Cover the work area with newspaper.
- Prepare a clean-up bowl or bucket with warm, soapy water.

Recipe for a little Creep (enough for a small group):

In a paper cup, mix 1 tablespoon of white glue with 2 teaspoons of water.

In another cup, mix 2 teaspoons of water with 1/2 teaspoon of borax. It won't dissolve completely. Swirl it around in the cup to keep it mixed.

While stirring the glue mixture, pour in the borax-water mixture.

Stir until the mixture gels, and then knead it like bread dough. You've created Creep.

Wash your hands.

Recipe for a lot of Creep:

Mix 2 cups of white glue with 1 1/2 cups of water. Combine 1/3 cup of water with 1 tablespoon of borax, and then continue as above.

- Before moving to the next step, explore the properties of Creep.

Supplies

- *newspaper*
- *large bowl or bucket*
- *water*
- *soap*
- *paper cups, 3 ounce*
- *measuring spoons and cups*
- *white glue*
- *laundry borax*
- *plastic spoons or wide popsicle sticks*
- *pencils*
- *scratch paper*
- *ruler*
- *paper towels*
- *copies of Design Briefs #1–#4*
- *safety glasses recommended*

- The challenge for your family is to develop and market a new product based on Creep. You'll learn about the needs and requirements of the product the same way an industrial chemist would—by reading a design brief and conducting experiments and tests.

- Read the 4 attached *Design Briefs* (see pages 154-155) that describe requirements for new products.

- Select a product to develop. Your group may want to work in smaller teams to develop more than one product.

- Following the guidelines and specifications outlined in the *Design Briefs*, create a version of Creep to meet your specifications. Have someone keep notes of your test results as you work.

- Once you have a product that meets the specifications of your design brief, write a Product Report to describe the product development. (You could write your report in your journal.) Be sure to include the following information:

  Product Report for Design Brief #___
  Development Team Members
  Product Manufacturing Instructions (for instance, "Use a maximum of 4 ounces of glue during development.")
  Product Ingredients (list ingredients, describe mixing procedures)
  Product Profile (name, packaging, description, distribution, target customer)
  Estimated Cost per Unit
  Production Time per Unit

- Share your product report, and demonstrate your product for the rest of your group.

Next

- Design a television commercial to advertise your product. Can you come up with a jingle?

- Invite a career guest who works in product development to visit a FAMILY SCIENCE class.

- Plan a field trip to an industrial research or production facility.

Design Brief #1: Recreation

Design a product that will be used for games of skill. The development goal is to produce a material that rolls and bounces. It must hold its shape after repeated use. The product may range in size from 1 to 2 inches (2.5 to 5 centimeters). Marketing opportunities include schools, science museums, toy shop, and carnivals.

The ability to produce large quantities at low cost is a priority. The primary handlers of the product will be untrained temporary workers. Frequent worker turnover requires a safe, easy-to-use product. In the workplace, the product will be handled in large quantities. The consumer will handle the product one at a time.

The manufacturing schedule must accommodate seasonal demand. Packaging and distribution must be designed for locations with limited facilities. The product must be transported on demand to rural and urban sites nationwide. Attention to disposal issues and environmental impact is essential. Reducing, reusing and recycling whenever possible is a top priority.

Design Brief #2: Collection

Design a product that will be used for collecting and storing samples for investigations. The development goal is to produce a flexible, adhesive material for use by professionals. The ability to mix it quickly on-site is a priority. Marketing opportunities include field researchers, law enforcement professionals and archaeologists.

The product must be able to be dispensed in small quantities and then stored until the investigation is complete. The primary handlers of the product will be on-site investigators who are highly skilled. In the laboratory, the technicians will handle only premixed samples. Frequent use requires a safe, easy-to-use product.

Manufacturing must accommodate quarterly purchases. Packaging and distribution of the product must meet the needs of investigators in technical, legal and scientific occupations. The product will be distributed internationally. Attention to disposal issues and environmental impact is essential. Reducing, reusing and recycling whenever possible is a top priority.

Design Brief #3: Modeling Material

Design a product that will be used to make 3-D maps and models. The development goal is to produce a flowing, elastic medium that hardens when dry for use by landscapers, geographers, map makers (cartographers) and land-use planners. Marketing opportunities include professional schools, governmental agencies and consulting firms.

The product must be able to be mixed in a range of quantities. The product must be able to be stored for short periods of time in the flowing state and long periods of time in the hardened state. The consumers of this product are skilled, technical workers. Prolonged contact with the skin requires a safe product.

The manufacturing schedule must accommodate consistent year-round use by professionals with occasional high demand cycles. Packaging and distribution of the product must appeal to designers and technicians. The product will be primarily used by agencies located in urban areas with a small, target audience. Attention to disposal issues and environmental impact is essential. Reducing, reusing and recycling whenever possible is a top priority.

Design Brief #4: Measuring Unit

Design a product that will be used to measure the capacity and volume of irregular containers or spaces. The development goal is to produce a non-sticky, easily reshaped material. Marketing opportunities include manufacturing, design firms and schools. The ability to quickly increase and decrease the amount of material is a priority.

The product must be able to be premixed in standard or metric units. The premixed samples will be reshaped frequently. The primary handlers of the product will be technicians, line workers, sorters or students. Frequent handling requires a clean and safe product.

The manufacturing schedule must accommodate a large quantity of one-time purchases and a limited home market. Packaging and distribution of the product will be through catalog and mail order outlets. Attention to disposal issues and environmental impact is essential. Reducing, reusing and recycling whenever possible is a top priority.

Balloon Rocket Enterprise

Why

To design and build models.
To conduct an experiment.

What

A cause is the reason something happens. The effect is the result of something happening. Our understanding about cause and effect increases through experience. In this activity, you'll explore a simple cause and effect relationship as you experiment with a balloon rocket. You will also re-design your rocket to see if you can improve its performance.

How

- Cut the *Balloon Rocket Enterprise* cards apart (see page 158).

- Read over each card, and arrange them in the order you will follow to do the activity.

- Find an open space to test your balloon rockets. Follow the steps on the *Balloon Rocket Enterprise* cards.

- In your journal, record any ideas or questions your family or group has while you are working.

Next

- After building a successful design, write a set of direction cards for someone else to follow to make your design.

- Find one way for a balloon rocket to do work for you, save you time, or accomplish a task.

Supplies

- *copy of the Balloon Rocket Enterprise directions*

- *scissors*

- *balloons, round, 6-10 inches*

- *felt pen*

- *string, at least 10 yards (11 meters)*

- *yardstick or meterstick*

- *plastic straw*

- *paper*

- *safety glasses recommended*

Balloon Rocket Enterprise

- Cut a piece of string about 10 yards (11 meters) long.

- Thread the string through the straw.

- Tape the straw to the balloon.

- Rockets travel through space using fuels that are burned to produce gas. The gases moving out the rocket's rear vents cause the rocket to move forward. In a balloon rocket, air escaping causes the balloon to move.

- Blow air into the balloon, and then hold it closed.

- Try this activity in groups of 3 or more.

- Build a balloon rocket using the following supplies:

balloon	meter tape
felt pen	plastic straw
a ball of string	masking tape
scissors	

- Measure and record the distance each design travels in trial #1. Repeat the measurement in trial #2.

model	Trial #1 distance	Trial #2 distance	Average
first design			
second design			
third design			

- To calculate the average distance, add the 2 trial distances, and then divide the total by 2.

- Write your name on the balloon.

- Broken balloon pieces can be harmful to living things. If a balloon breaks, put all the broken pieces in a trash bag to prevent living things from swallowing them.

- Continue designing and testing balloon rockets, trying 1 change at a time.

- Test each design 2 times.

- Pull the string taut. (Taut means tightly stretched.)

- When you release the balloon, it will move. The balloon moves opposite the direction of the escaping air. This demonstrates one of Issac Newton's laws of motion: for every action, there is an equal and opposite reaction.

- List ideas about how to increase the distance the balloon rocket moves along the string.

_____

_____

- Modify your rocket and test it again.

Balloon Rocket Enterprise

293

Supplies

- *popcorn kernels*
- *hot air popcorn popper*
- *pot holder*
- *heatproof bowl*
- *pencil*
- *tape*
- *construction paper*
- *scissors*
- *paper towels*
- *felt pen*

Why

To compare and classify materials.
To estimate volumes.

Who

In 1948, scientists exploring the Bat Cave in New Mexico discovered that American Indians had lived there for more than three thousand years. Research revealed that American Indians were the first people to cultivate corn, and popcorn was one of their earliest foods. Popcorn kernels discovered at Bat Cave were carbon dated to 2000 BC. Researchers uncovered 766 corn cobs, 293 popcorn kernels, and 6 popped kernels.

What

Take a close look at a handful of popcorn kernels. They can be classified into two primary types: rice and pearl. Rice kernels are long, flat, and pointed with dented sides. Pearl kernels are short with smooth, rounded crowns. The shiny outside covering of a popcorn kernel is called the pericarp. This hard covering splits when the kernel is heated. For the best popping results, the moisture inside the kernel should be between 13.5% and 15.5%. When it pops, the starchy, white substance inside the kernel called the endosperm expands. After popping, popcorn can be sorted into groups based on appearance. The smaller, compact popcorn with the pericarp still clustered together is the mushroom type. The butterfly type popcorn is larger and more open, with smaller, broken pieces of pericarp.

How

In this activity, your family or group will sort and classify popcorn types, and you'll design a container to hold 293 popped kernels.

- Select a few kernels to observe and compare. Use the description of rice and pearl kernels to find 1 of each type.

- Pop a small batch of popcorn. Sort the popped popcorn into groups based on shape and size. Try to identify both the mushroom and butterfly types of popped corn.

Design Brief: Design
a container to hold 293
popped kernels of corn.

- Make a chart to record unpopped kernel and popped popcorn observations.

- Next, discuss methods for counting a 293 kernel sample.

- Before popping the corn, discuss how much space each person predicts the 293 popcorn kernels will fill after popping.

- Have each individual use tape and paper to design and build his/her own container to hold the popped corn. The finished container should have room for all of the popcorn without any empty space or any popcorn overflowing the container.

- Pour 293 kernels into a preheated popper. Use a heatproof container to catch the popped corn.

- Once cooled, pour the popped corn into each paper container. Who's container was closest to the right size?

Next

- Hot air poppers typically have a 1/2 cup dispenser which holds approximately 700-800 kernels. How many cups of popped popcorn will a hot air popper with a full dispenser produce? Build a container that will hold the 1/2 cup of kernels after they've popped. Measure the container and calculate its volume (length x width x depth).

Chute

Supplies

- *masking tape*
- *paper and pen*
- *scissors*
- *an assortment of empty containers (for example, cereal boxes, paper towel rolls, milk cartons, bags and trays)*
- *marbles*
- *safety glasses recommended*

Why

To experiment with potential and kinetic energy by designing and constructing a chute.

What

Technology is the application of knowledge, tools, and skills to solve practical problems; in this case, controlling and guiding the movement of an object down a chute. For example, a special kind of chute called a flume is used to move water, logs or both between high and low points. Your family will design and construct a chute using recycled containers to move a marble from high to low.

In this activity, gravitational potential energy is converted into kinetic energy. Kinetic energy is the energy an object has when it is in motion. Potential energy is the stored energy that can be converted into another form. Each time you place a marble at the top of a chute it has gravitational potential energy. Once the marble begins to roll down the chute it demonstrates kinetic energy. Gravity is the force providing this kinetic energy.

How

> Design Brief: Design a chute with at least 5 sections through which a marble will move from the top to the bottom of a vertical surface.

- Choose a smooth vertical surface that won't be damaged by sticking and removing tape. Try the refrigerator, a door, shower wall, or basement wall.

- Decide exactly how high on the wall you want to start, and then make a "start" sign to hang there. Write "stop" on a container with an open top. Place it on the floor next to the wall not directly underneath your start sign. Now construct your chute.

- Each container for the chute needs 2 openings: one opening for the marble to roll in, and the other for the marble to roll out.

- Position the first container on the wall, and attach it to the wall with tape.

- Continue attaching containers to the wall until you have a chute with at least 5 sections connecting start to stop.

- Periodically drop in the marble to check the chute's path while you work.

- Draw a picture of your completed chute. How long does it take for a marble to drop through all 5 sections of the chute. Can you shorten or lengthen the drop time?

CHAPTER 8

ORGANIZING A FAMILY SCIENCE EVENT

FAMILY SCIENCE isn't just a book. It's a whole program for families. It's a way for adults and children to work side by side, learning and enjoying science.

What is a FAMILY SCIENCE event?

A FAMILY SCIENCE event could be a special evening of fun science activities for families. It could also be a series of classes where families attend 3 or more workshops, or a Saturday neighborhood event where children and adults explore and discover science topics together.

Who can do a FAMILY SCIENCE event?

Anyone can! Parents, teachers, school administrators, community members, clergy, science professionals, or anyone else who has an interest in encouraging parents and children to enjoy science together.

Where do FAMILY SCIENCE events take place?

FAMILY SCIENCE events can be done anywhere: school cafeterias, community centers, scouting facilities, church basements, at home or, if the weather cooperates, even outdoors.

Who attends a FAMILY SCIENCE event?

FAMILY SCIENCE is intended to serve all family members—moms, dads, kids, grandparents, aunts, uncles, cousins, whoever! The key is that adults and children work together. The group doesn't need to be big. Working with just two or three families is a good way to start.

Why do a FAMILY SCIENCE event?

It's fun! You're never too old to learn, and a FAMILY SCIENCE event gives parents and children the chance to learn together. Families doing science together can:

- bridge the gap that often exists between home and school.
- change attitudes about who does science and what science is.
- address anxiety about science being too hard or nerdy.
- break down the stereotypes about who does science.
- lay the foundation for improving other basic skills, like communication, reading and mathematics.

How do I get started doing a FAMILY SCIENCE event?

This chapter can help you organize an event in your community. Our goal is to take you step-by-step through the process of planning, implementing and wrapping-up a successful FAMILY SCIENCE event.

Resources And Funding

Before you start planning your FAMILY SCIENCE event, you'll want to round up some help. Brainstorm a list of what you'll need and people you know who may be available for your event. For instance, colleagues or parents may be willing to join a planning committee. If you need financial assistance or donations for supplies, consider approaching local businesses who have supported you in the past or appear to have an interest in science education. Local teenagers can help out by being mentors to young explorers or by providing day care for very young children during your event.

When asking an individual or group for support, be clear and concise. Explain what event you are planning and why you think that FAMILY SCIENCE is important for your community. Outline exactly what you need (volunteers, money, donated supplies, etc.) and how this individual/group can help. If someone is offering a large donation (money or materials) offer to acknowledge their support on your flyers, at the event, and in any media releases you distribute. After the event is over, all of your helpers deserve a heartfelt thank-you note.

The following list offers ideas about where you might find support for your FAMILY SCIENCE event(s).

Sources for volunteers

- FAMILY SCIENCE instructors
- High school service groups/clubs
- Local college students
- Fraternities/sororities
- Local civic groups (Rotary, Kiwanis)
- Science or Nature Centers
- Local PTA/PTO
- Scout troops
- Boys/Girls Clubs
- Local businesses
- Teenagers
- Retired citizens' groups

Sources for financial help or in-kind donations:

- Local foundations
- Local businesses
- State Department of Education
- Grants
- Tribal council funds
- After-school program fees
- Neighborhood Associations
- Eisenhower funds for teacher training
- Church, synagogue, other places of worship
- PTA/PTO
- School principal
- School district
- Community action funds
- Fraternities/sororities
- Retired citizens' groups

Reaching Your Audience

Who is the audience for your FAMILY SCIENCE event?

There may be an easy answer to this question, or you may have to think a bit about who you'd like to serve. Decide who your audience will be first, and then go on to other areas of planning.

Once you have decided on your target audience, the next challenge is getting them to the event. The following list offers some strategies for how to reach families and motivate them to attend FAMILY SCIENCE.

Consider time and location carefully.

Making the time convenient for families is very important, but also consider where the event will be held. Don't choose a location that is remote, intimidating or unsafe. Combining your event with another activity might provide further incentive to participate. For instance, schedule the event to follow a church service, soccer game, parent conferences, scout troop meeting or other group activity. Choose a location that is easy to find, provides a pleasant learning atmosphere and is inexpensive or free.

Contact people one-on-one.

Inviting each family individually will yield the greatest number of participants. Be persuasive, excited and encouraging when you talk to families. Use teachers, principals, clergy members, other parents, tutors, teacher aides, PTA volunteers, older children and anyone else you can think of to help deliver personal invitations.

Offer incentives to participate.

There is no shortage of creative ways to motivate families:

- Offer prizes.
- Provide baby-sitting for very young children.
- Provide transportation to and from the event/classes.
- Encourage teachers to give students a break from homework or award extra credit for attending the event.
- Invite a well-known speaker or special guest to the event.
- Advertise the number of quality family hours participants will enjoy.

Serve food.

People always respond to "free" food! Offer simple snacks or organize a barbecue. Whatever you chose, be sure to mention the availability of food in your advertising.

Publicize your event.

The next section offers a number of suggestions for how to get the word out about your upcoming FAMILY SCIENCE event.

Publicizing a FAMILY SCIENCE Event

Once you've identified the target audience for your event, you'll need to come up with a plan for publicity. Think about publicity in the early planning stages, so you have plenty of time to create materials and distribute them in advance of your event. Perhaps you can recruit a volunteer with public relations or marketing skills to help you.

Key Messages

Before you send out any publicity, identify your key messages. All publicity should contain the basic information below so that families can get excited about the event and will know just what to expect.

- Who is it for? (*an event for the entire family*)

- What is the event? (*a fun-filled evening, a series of hands-on activities, classes, etc.*)

- When is it being held? (*day of the week, date, time*)

- Where is it being held? (*name of building, street address, city*)

- Why should people come? (*for quality family time, to learn about science, to do hands-on activities, etc.*)

- How do you sign up? (*return a pre-registration form, call the event coordinator*)

- Sponsors and/or fee (*be sure to publicize the names of your sponsors or, if there's a fee to attend, make sure that you state it*)

Types of Publicity

An event designed for a small group of neighborhood families may only require that a school flyer be sent home and follow-up calls be made before the event. If you're trying to reach a larger audience, however, you may want to distribute posters, send a direct mailing, and notify local media. Whatever route you take, keep in mind who you're trying to reach and what message you want them to hear.

The samples in this chapter can be copied and customized for your own use or used to get your creative juices flowing. Remember to make your publicity eye-catching by using color, artwork, or a unique design, and keep the number of words to a minimum.

Flyers – Route your FAMILY SCIENCE event flyers through neighborhood schools, send them to civic and youth organizations to post on bulletin boards or attach to their monthly newsletters, blanket cars in a parking lot (be sure to get permission from whoever owns the lot), place a stack in the local library, or go door-to-door. (See the sample flyer on page 171.)

Posters – Distribute colorful posters to schools, grocery stores, libraries, storefronts, churches, etc. Think of places where members of your target audience will most likely see them.

Direct Mail – If you have access to a mailing list of families, you may want to consider sending personal invitations. The local school or neighborhood association may be able to provide such a list.

Phone Calls – Never underestimate the power of direct contact! Recruit volunteers, or assign members of your event planning committee to personally call and invite at least 5 families they know. Or, you may want to restrict your phone calls to reminding just those families who have pre-registered for your event.

Media – Before you send notices about your event to the media, determine what it is you have to offer them as news. Small events or classes for local families may be of interest to a community or school newspaper. Larger events with lots of people and lots of action may attract a regional newspaper or magazine, or even the local evening news. Most media like stories with kids, television reporters need something to look at, and a radio station will want a story that can be told with spoken words, music and other interesting sounds. And remember, all media have deadlines, so be prepared to work within them. (See sample *Media Advisory* and *FAMILY SCIENCE Fact Sheet* on pages 172-173.)

Thank-You's – Most of us think about publicity before an event, but what you do after the event is important as well. Be sure to send thank-you's to volunteers, sponsors, guest presenters, donors, and any media that showed up. Show your appreciation for their efforts, and let them know you may be calling them again for your next FAMILY SCIENCE event! (See sample *Thank-you* on page 188.)

Looking for a new and different way to spend time with your family?

Then check out...

FAMILY SCIENCE!

* Work as a family and build your science skills.

* Try hands-on activities that make learning fun.

* Free admission. Treats!

* All ages welcome.

Date:
Time:
Place:

FAMILY SCIENCE is sponsored by:

MEDIA ADVISORY

For More Information
Contact: [NAME]
                 [PHONE NUMBER]
                 [E-mail]

KIDS + ADULTS + SCIENCE = FUN AND GAMES FOR EVERYONE!
[Name of school or group] Hosts Science Event For Local Families

[YOUR CITY, STATE] – Adults and kids of all ages will gather at [LOCATION] on [DAY OF WEEK, MONTH, DAY] from [TIME] for a very special [DAY, EVENING, WEEKEND] filled with creative, hands-on science activities. This FAMILY SCIENCE event is part of a national educational outreach program designed to encourage parents and children to explore and discover science together. The program also seeks to increase the number of students in kindergarten through 8th grade who enjoy science and who can apply science concepts to everyday life.

FAMILY SCIENCE events and classes always feature creative, cooperative hands-on learning activities. The activities use common, inexpensive materials and are designed to complement the concepts taught in current school science curriculum.

Local sponsors of this FAMILY SCIENCE event include [LIST NAMES OF INDIVIDUAL OR COMPANY SPONSORS].

FAMILY SCIENCE FACT SHEET

For More Information
Contact: [NAME]
                [PHONE NUMBER]
                [E-MAIL]

What: A FAMILY SCIENCE event featuring fun, cooperative hands-on science activities for K-8 students and their families.

When: [DAY OF WEEK, MONTH, DAY, YEAR]
            [TIME]

Where: [NAME OF LOCATION]
            [STREET ADDRESS]

Why: To give local families the opportunity to work together and discover new ways of learning about science. FAMILY SCIENCE seeks to increase the number of students who study science in grades K-8, particularly those typically underrepresented in science-based careers.

Cost: The program is free to the public. Refreshments will be provided.

Who: Local sponsors of the event include X, Y, & Z.

FAMILY SCIENCE is a national science program that encourages parents and children of all ages to work together as they tinker, test ideas and talk about science. Local families can participate in FAMILY SCIENCE through special events or classes held in their community.

The FAMILY SCIENCE Event

There are common elements to consider when planning any type of FAMILY SCIENCE event. This section offers help with initial planning, event registration, scheduling, evaluation, and thanking those who helped to make the event a success. There is also a suggested timeline to follow.

Initial Planning

The most successful FAMILY SCIENCE events will be coordinated by a group of people, not just one individual. Working as a team helps to spread out the tasks and responsibilities and shares ownership with more people. If people feel like they have been part of the process, they will be more likely to help promote your event, recruit others, and participate fully.

Use the following *FAMILY SCIENCE Event Planning Sheet* (page 175) as a guide for you and your team. Make sure that you have thought through each phase of your event and have assigned someone to be responsible for each section. Once completed, the *Event Planning Sheet* will be a valuable tool to use before, during and after your FAMILY SCIENCE event.

FAMILY SCIENCE Event Planning Planning Sheet

Date(s): _____   Time: _____

Location: _____   Phone: _____

Event Leader(s) (name, phone): _____

Time	Things To Be Done		Who	Where
Set-up				
Openers*				
Welcome/Introduction				
Activity Session(s)*				
Closing/Evaluations				
Clean-up				

*Attach a supply list for each activity.

Event Registration

In most cases, you will want to know who is planning to attend your event. This is helpful for a variety of reasons:

- You can plan for the appropriate amount of space, supplies and refreshments.

- You can target your event more accurately to the participants (age level, interests, etc.).

- You can meet any special needs participants might have (translators, handicap access, extra seats for senior participants, etc.).

A sample *Registration Form* (see page 177) is useful to collect data on those families planning to attend your event. This form can be used on its own, or you can combine it with the sample tri-fold *Invitations* (see pages 178-179).

Join us for FAMILY SCIENCE!

What?   FAMILY SCIENCE is an exciting program for children and adults who want to have fun and explore science by doing hands-on activities. Family members test, tinker, and learn about science in daily life, school, and work. FAMILY SCIENCE demonstrates that science is everywhere and for everybody's family!

When?

Where?

To register your family for FAMILY SCIENCE, fill in the form below and return to:

✂ -

Yes! Sign us up for FAMILY SCIENCE!

No. of Adults: _____   No. of Children: _____

Name(s): _____   Name(s)& Age(s): _____

_____   _____

The best way/time to reach our family is: _____   _____

_____   _____

Signature: _____   _____

Find out at FAMILY SCIENCE

More information inside

SHOULD PARENTS BE USED IN SCIENCE EXPERIMENTS?

WONDERING
WHAT
TO DO?

How about
FAMILY SCIENCE?

Open for details.

Event Schedule

The schedule that you choose for your event can vary. Most successful events are between 1 and 2 hours long. Events longer than this may require too great of a commitment on the part of the families.

Page 181 contains a *Sample Schedule* for a FAMILY SCIENCE event. This sample could be adapted for either a one-time event or a series of classes.

As you dive into the activities, remember to keep safety in mind. Review the section on *Safe Learning* on page 20. Depending on your group, you may want to use a *Safety Contract* (see page 182). You can use it as it is, or you can customize your own using the blank *Safety Contract* template on page 183. Regardless of how you choose to focus on safety, make sure that the message is clear to all participants: A fun activity is a safe one!

Sample Schedule

Evening Event from 7:00–8:30pm

6:00 Set-up
Set up opener activity tables around the room
Set up supply table for regular activities
Prepare welcome table (set out supplies for nametags, post sign-in sheets, etc.)
Hang any signage
Prepare refreshments

6:45 Welcome Table
Staff for early arrivals
Have participants make nametags and sign-in

7:00 Openers
Offer 3 or 4 different openers
Have 2–3 copies of each activity available so multiple families can work at the same time

7:20 Welcome and Introductions
Introduce staff, volunteers and special guests
Review agenda
Orient participants to the facility (restrooms, refreshments, etc.)
Outline program goals

7:30 Activity Sessions

8:20 Wrap-up
Hand out evaluations
Assign homework (if there will be another session)
Suggest ways to keep learning science as a family at home
Offer closing remarks
Thank participants for coming

8:30 Clean-up
Invite family participation
Divide up responsibilities
De-brief staff and volunteers
Review evaluations

Safety Contract

Activity/Activities	Class	Date

The safety rules for this activity are:

Work with an adult partner.

Stay in the designated work area.

Listen, read, and follow directions.

Identify and label substances in use.

Don't taste anything.

Clean up spills immediately.

Keep equipment, materials and fingers away from eyes and mouth.

Use tools and materials correctly.

Report any injuries immediately.

Ask questions if you're not sure what to do.

Wash your hands at the end of the activity.

We, the following people, agree to think about safety first when working with tools, materials, and other people during this activity.

Safety Contract

Activity/Activities   **Class**   **Date**

The safety rules for this activity are:

We, the following people, agree to think about safety first when working with tools, materials, and other people during this activity.

_____   _____

_____   _____

_____   _____

_____   _____

Nametags

Using nametags is a good idea for any FAMILY SCIENCE event. They help you identify and call people by name, and they help participants get to know each other. Making nametags at the beginning of class can also provide an opportunity to demonstrate how science surrounds us in our daily lives. First names, in large letters, work the best!

Here are some fun, science-filled nametag-making ideas:

Metric Measure

Cut a length of string as long as your arm from your shoulder to your fingertips. Use a meter stick to measure the string. Record the length on the corner of your nametag and write your name in the middle. Use tape to attach the string to your nametag. Now you can wear it.

Coded Nametags

Use a code to write your name. You can make up a code or use an existing one such as Morse Code or Braille.

Mirror

Place your nametag in front of a mirror and write your name while looking in the mirror. (Mirror images are reversed. They transpose left with right and right with left.) Wear your nametag. Now use a mirror to read others' names.

Tied Up In Knots

Write your name on an index card. Cut a string as long as your arm. Punch 1 hole in your card. Thread the string through the hole. Use a fancy knot to secure your nametag. (Consult a dictionary or encyclopedia for pictures of unusual knots.)

Handful

Trace your hand on a sheet of paper and cut it out. Add fingerprints to each of the fingers of the hand. To do this, rub a pencil on a sheet of paper. Rub your fingertip over the area until the graphite covers your fingerprint. Working with your partner, attach a short length of tape to your fingertip and press it down. Lift the piece of tape and attach it to the matching paper fingertip.

There are a number of different fingerprint types: loop, plain arch, tented arch, double loop, central pocket loop, plain whorl, accidental whorl. Write your name on the palm of your paper hand. Attach your hand-shaped nametag with tape or a string.

Evaluation

We all benefit from feedback. Taking the time to ask participants for their input after your FAMILY SCIENCE event will let you know what went well and can help you improve future events. If the event was a success, sponsors will enjoy hearing specific details about the event, and documenting the success will help in getting future support.

The next page is a sample evaluation form to distribute to participants. You can simply copy and distribute this form, or you can make one of your own. Remember to keep it short and simple for the best response, and be sure to give participants plenty of time to fill it out. If they are rushed, their answers will not be as thorough as you may want.

FAMILY SCIENCE Evaluation

Date of Event:_____

Location:_____

We're always interested in improving our FAMILY SCIENCE event.
Thank you for taking a few moments to complete this form.

	Strongly Disagree				Strongly Agree
The directions for the activities were easy to follow.	1	2	3	4	5
It was confusing.	1	2	3	4	5
There was plenty of time to do each activity.	1	2	3	4	5
I felt rushed.	1	2	3	4	5
I learned activities I can do at home with my child.	1	2	3	4	5
I talked with others about science.	1	2	3	4	5
I enjoyed myself.	1	2	3	4	5
It was worthwhile.	1	2	3	4	5
It was disappointing.	1	2	3	4	5
I would attend another event.	1	2	3	4	5
I would recommend this event to a friend.	1	2	3	4	5

One suggestion for improving this FAMILY SCIENCE event is:

Anything else you want us to know?

Write additional comments on the back.

- -

FAMILY SCIENCE Evaluation

Date of Event:_____

Location:_____

We're always interested in improving our FAMILY SCIENCE event.
Thank you for taking a few moments to complete this form.

	Strongly Disagree				Strongly Agree
The directions for the activities were easy to follow.	1	2	3	4	5
It was confusing.	1	2	3	4	5
There was plenty of time to do each activity.	1	2	3	4	5
I felt rushed.	1	2	3	4	5
I learned activities I can do at home with my child.	1	2	3	4	5
I talked with others about science.	1	2	3	4	5
I enjoyed myself.	1	2	3	4	5
It was worthwhile.	1	2	3	4	5
It was disappointing.	1	2	3	4	5
I would attend another event.	1	2	3	4	5
I would recommend this event to a friend.	1	2	3	4	5

One suggestion for improving this FAMILY SCIENCE event is:

Anything else you want us to know?

Write additional comments on the back.

- -

Wrap-up

The event is over and everyone says it was a smashing success. You still have a very important task remaining: to thank all those folks who helped you. Taking the time to thank your supporters will promote interest in future projects and make everyone more excited about the next FAMILY SCIENCE event. Here are some people you may want to put on your list:

- FAMILY SCIENCE planning team

- FAMILY SCIENCE participants

- FAMILY SCIENCE instructors

- Career guests

- Volunteers

- Facility owner/administrator

- School personnel (administrators, school board members, teachers, teacher aides, janitors or facility managers)

- Sponsors/donors

See page 188 for a sample tri-fold *Thank-you*. You can either copy this form and hand-write your thanks, or you can type a thank-you note and copy it onto the back.

Page 189 offers a blank FAMILY SCIENCE participation certificate. Use it for event participants, presenters, helpers or anyone else who deserves a little something special.

Thanks for helping us find it
at FAMILY SCIENCE.

SCIENCE IS EVERYWHERE!

This certifies that the following family members

_____

participated in FAMILY SCIENCE

at _____

on _____

_____

FAMILY SCIENCE

Getting Ready Checklist

Three to six months in advance:

❏ Identify the audience you want to reach for your event or classes.
❏ Choose a date (have 2-3 options).
❏ Secure a location, and be sure to consider the following:
  occupancy limit
  accessibility to public transportation, availability of parking space
  security issues
  access to kitchen & restroom facilities, handicap accessibility
  availability of tables, chairs, and other supplies
❏ Put together an event planning committee.
❏ Devise a strategy for publicizing your event. Consider:
  school & community flyers
  community calendars (print & broadcast)
  direct mail, signs/posters

Two to three months in advance:

❏ Choose a theme/topics for your event.
❏ Draft a list of potential activities. Try them out.
❏ Make up a schedule.
❏ Do some preliminary advertising.
❏ Contact potential guest presenters.

Three to four weeks in advance:

❏ Distribute pre-registration flyers and other publicity materials.
❏ Finalize your event schedule.
❏ Organize and prepare materials/supplies, evaluations.
❏ Recruit assistants for the event.

One to two weeks in advance:

❏ Send reminders or make follow-up calls to pre-registered families.
❏ Confirm guest presenters.
❏ Arrange for access to the event location (if held after-hours).
❏ Send media advisories.
❏ Arrange for refreshments.

After the event:

❏ Send thank-you notes.
❏ Congratulate yourself on a job well done!

APPENDIX

Science Learning for Everyone

One of the goals of FAMILY SCIENCE is to get kids more excited about science and technology. Children are often naturally curious about science, but the ways we communicate and act sometimes discourages that curiosity before it can flourish. Subtle messages from parents, teachers and other adults can convince some students that science isn't for them. You can help remove obstacles to science learning for your own children by trying some of the following suggestions:

Raise your expectations.

Research shows that children tend to perform to the level of the expectations placed on them by teachers, parents, and adult mentors. Set high expectations for your children and help them to accomplish their goals.

Encourage questions.

Curious adults ask questions, and kids are no different. When children ask questions, they are trying to develop models and explanations for what they see around them. This is exactly what scientists do. Encourage your child to ask questions, and don't be afraid if you don't know the answers. Scientists don't know all the answers either. That's why they investigate!

Emphasize future education.

Help your children see the value of education by showing them that you value it, too. Even if you did not complete your own education, you can still show your children that you think education is important by talking with their teachers, asking about homework, and attending school functions.

Use stuff.

One of the fun things about science is all the neat tools and gizmos that are associated with scientific study. When doing science activities, make sure your children have plenty of materials to work with. Most supplies aren't expensive and can be found around your home.

Encourage creativity.

When a child shows interest in a topic, encourage him/her to pursue that interest as far as possible. Check out books from the library, talk to friends, teachers, family members and neighbors about it. Help your child to build models, draw pictures or write about his/her particular interest. When one interest passes, move on to the next one!

Eliminate negativity.

All children need good self-esteem to be successful no matter what field of study they pursue. Eliminate any negative talk about science and math from your vocabulary and your children's. Some examples include parents saying, "I hated math when I was a kid," or children teasing each other about becoming a "science nerd."

Discuss the accomplishments of "non-traditional" scientists.

Fortunately, we have more opportunities everyday to expose children to scientists who come from underrepresented groups. Talk about what scientists do and point out scientists who defy stereotypes.

Connect with role models.

Children learn by example. Meeting and talking with people from a variety of backgrounds and careers opens your children's eyes to their own potential in the future.

Visit science places.

Take your children to visit museums, science centers, zoos, botanical gardens, planetariums and nature centers. Offer to take friends and other family members, too.

FAMILY SCIENCE and the National Science Education Standards

In 1996, the National Research Council published a landmark document, the *National Science Education Standards*. The *Standards* offer a contemporary definition of what it means to be scientifically literate, and they reflect the new ways that both scientists and educators are thinking about science education. The *Standards* are designed for students, teachers, administrators, science educators, parents and other policy makers to help guide their decisions about what to include in science education programs.

Many of the goals of FAMILY SCIENCE mirror the principles set forth by the *Standards*. For instance, the *Standards* state that learning is an active process. "Learning is something that students do, not something that is done to them" (*National Science Education Standards*, page 2). Hands-on and, more importantly, minds-on experiences are essential for students. Clearly, FAMILY SCIENCE is not filled with lectures on science content. Instead, FAMILY SCIENCE encourages participants to "get their hands dirty" doing science and challenges them to think about the reasons and causes for the phenomena they witness.

The *Standards* also lay out basic science content that students should master at each grade-level in school. The content standards touch on traditional divisions of scientific study, such as physical science, life science and earth and space science. They also include less conventional content standards, such as the history and nature of science and science in personal and social perspectives. The fundamental goal is that students gain mastery of the content standards at each level. However, the hope is that many students' curiosity will draw them deeper into particular areas of study, taking them beyond the basics.

FAMILY SCIENCE complements the content standards by touching on many of the topics listed above. For example, one of the content standards for K-4 physical science states: "Objects are made of one or more materials, such as paper, wood or metal. Objects can be described by the properties of the materials from which they are made, and those properties can be used to separate or sort a group of objects or materials" (*Standards*, page 126). In Common Properties (page X), families work together to sort groups of objects based on their properties. They can sort a miscellaneous group of objects based on whether they

FAMILY SCIENCE

roll or slide down an inclined plane or sink or float in water. The behaviors of the objects, when tested, offers insights into the materials used to make them and helps families to understand similarities and differences as they sort the objects.

Another hallmark of the *Standards* is its emphasis on inquiry-based learning. As the *Standards* describe it:

> Inquiry is central to science learning. When engaging in inquiry, students describe objects and events, ask questions, construct explanations, test those explanations against current scientific knowledge, and communicate their ideas to others. They identify their assumptions, use critical and logical thinking, and consider alternative explanations. In this way, students actively develop their understanding of science by combining scientific knowledge with reasoning and thinking skills (*Standards*, page 2).

Inquiry is at the heart of FAMILY SCIENCE. Beyond just hands-on activities, FAMILY SCIENCE encourages families to work together to make discoveries about science, to talk about those discoveries and to learn more about what they have experienced. Through FAMILY SCIENCE, families have the opportunity to build basic skills, such as communication and problem-solving, while deepening their own relationships and understanding of each other.

Lastly, the *Standards* emphasize that science is for everyone. "The *Standards* apply to all students, regardless of age, gender, cultural or ethnic background, disabilities, aspirations, or interest and motivation in science" (*Standards*, page 2). FAMILY SCIENCE helps to promote this emphasis by using scientifically sound activities that are also inviting to those who may not have been exposed to science in the past. Many activities also celebrate the scientific achievements of people from a variety of backgrounds by including historical information.

We invite you to read the new *Standards*. By doing so, you will see how the activities in FAMILY SCIENCE mesh with the direction of national science education reform. More importantly, through FAMILY SCIENCE events, you can help promote and support this transformation in your own community. "With distributed leadership and coordinated changes in practice among all who have responsibility for science education reform, advances in science education can rapidly accumulate and produce recognizable improvement in the scientific literacy of all students and future citizens" (*Standards*, page 244).

National Science Education Standards. National Academy Press, 1996.

Resources

Key:

P = Primary (PreK-3)
E = Elementary (4-6)
M = Middle School/Junior High (7-9)
* = Elementary and middle school students would enjoy reading these books.

P   Allen, Judy, Earldene McNeil, and Velma Schmidt. *Cultural Awareness for Children.* Addison-Wesley Publishing Company, 1997.

P   Bailey, Pam, Debby Cryer, Thelma Harms, Sheri Osborne, and Barbara A. Kniest. *Active Learning for Children with Disabilities.* Addison-Wesley Publishing Company, 1997.

PE   Baker, Gwendolyn C. *Planning and Organizing for Multicultural Instruction.* Addison-Wesley Publishing Company, 1994.

PEM   *Benchmarks for Scientific Literacy.* American Association for the Advancement of Science, 1993.

EM* Bernstein, Leonard, Alan Winkler, and Linda Zierdt-Warshaw. *Multicultural Women of Science.* Peoples Publishing Group, 1996.

PE   Butzow, Carol M. and John W. Butzow. *More Science through Children's Literature: An Integrated Approach.* Libraries Unlimited, 1998.

PEM   Bybee, Roger. *Achieving Science Literacy: From Purposes to Practices.* Heinemann, 1997.

PEM   Calkins, Lucy with Lydia Bellino. *Raising Lifelong Learners: A Parent's Guide.* Perseus Printing, 1997.

EM   Carey, Shelley J. *Science for All Cultures.* National Science Teacher's Association, 1993.

P   Coates, Grace Davila and Jean Kerr Stenmark. *Family Math for Young Children: Comparing.* University of California, 1997.

EM* Cooney, Miriam P. *Celebrating Women in Math and Science.* National Council of Teachers of Mathematics, 1996.

EM   Fraser, Sherry, Project Director. *SPACES: Solving Problems of Access to Careers in Engineering and Science.* Lawrence Hall of Science. Dale Seymour Publications, 1982.

FAMILY SCIENCE

E   Fredericks, Anthony D. *Letters to Parents in Science.* Goodyear Publishing Company, 1993.

P   Harlan, Jean Durgin and Mary S. Rivkin. *Science Experiences for the Early Childhood Years: An Integrated Approach.* Merrill Publishing Company, 1995.

PE   Jaffe, Roberta and Gary Appel. *The Growing Classroom: Garden-Based Science.* Addison-Wesley Publishing Company, 1996.

P   Lind, Karen K. *Exploring Science in Early Childhood.* Delmar Publishing, 1996.

EM*   Mundahl, John. *Tales of Courage, Tales of Dreams: A Multicultural Reader.* Addison-Wesley Publishing Company, 1993.

PEM   *National Science Education Standards.* National Academy Press, 1996.

E   Popelka, Susan. *Super Science with Simple Stuff: Activities for the Intermediate Grades.* Addison-Wesley Publishing Company, 1997.

EM*   Reimer, Luetta and Wilbert Reimer. *Mathematicians Are People, Too.* Dale Seymour Publications, 1990.

PEM   Russell, Helen Ross. *Ten Minute Field Trips.* National Science Teacher's Association, 1991.

PEM   Rutherford, F. James and Andrew Ahlgren. *Science for All Americans.* American Association for the Advancement of Science, 1990.

PEM   *Science for All Children.* National Science Resources Center, 1997.

PEM   Skolnick, Joan, Carol Langbort, and Lucille Day. *How to Encourage Girls in Math and Science.* Dale Seymour Publications, 1997.

PEM   Stenmark, Jean Kerr, Virginia Thompson, and Ruth Cossey. *Family Math.* University of California, 1986. (Also available in Spanish.)

PE   Strongin, Herb. *Science on a Shoestring.* Addison-Wesley Publishing Company, 1991.

M   Thompson, Virignia and Karen Mayfield-Ingram. *Family Math: the Middle School Years.* University of California, 1998.

EM*   VanCleve, Janice. *Science for Every Kid* series. (Variety of topics available including: Astronomy, Oceans, Physics, Chemistry, Human Body, Earth Science, etc.).

P   Winnett, David A., Robert A. Williams, Elizabeth A. Sherwood, and Robert E. Rockwell. *Discovery Science: Explorations for the Early Years.* Addison-Wesley Publishing Company, 1995.